Through the Eyes of One?

Kevin Hines

ISBN: 978-0-9910923-1-4
Copyright © Kevin Hines 2014
Published by:
CONVERPAGE
23 Acorn Street
Scituate, MA 02066

Introduction

Human behavior is fascinating. Seeing how one responds to certain situations can tell you a lot about that person. I do not claim to be an expert in human behavior. The readings in this book are solely my opinions and observations of the character of people. Give me a moment to introduce myself. My name is Kevin Hines and I have spent the last twenty five years training in the martial arts. In that time I have had the privilege of meeting many people. Through these meetings I have learned a lot about how one reacts or behaves to different situations. Although we are all unique, there are some common truths that are universal. Like most people, my life has been filled with highs and lows. But it is through these times that one learns much about themselves. The low times in my life were almost unbearable. I say this only to inform you that this book is not coming from someone who has had life handed to them. I have struggled and fought my entire life with only myself to rely on. Martial arts has been a best friend to me over the years. It has pushed me to be the very best I can be, not only in the training hall but also in all aspects of life. Recently I have created and founded my own martial arts system which was incredibly difficult and tedious, but through hard work and perseverance it is complete and I am very proud of the results. I have earned many ranks and degrees along the way, but what I have really earned is knowledge. Not only knowledge of myself but of others as well. The readings in this book are my thoughts and how I see life. I cannot promise that you have never heard words similar to these, maybe in a different text. I certainly understand that there are movies, songs, poems and all sorts of media where insightful quotes may have been said. It would be impossible to know everything that's ever been said by everybody. However, I can promise I have never heard them in the context that I have written them. Which is why I felt the need to write this book. These writings may be interpreted differently by different people. Some may agree with certain things and disagree with others. Or maybe have a completely unique opinion they would like to share. I am very interested in hearing peoples comments. So, on the back of every page there is a space for your own thoughts concerning each reading. Please feel free to write down your feelings or opinions. Or maybe how a particular page has effected your life or given you a different view on something going on now. You can share your thoughts in an open forum on our Facebook page. Please remember this is not meant to offend anyone or change your perspective. It is only to make you think, and if in the process it helps you or a loved one in any way then the effort of writing this book was worth it. When you have finished reading, you be the judge... are these opinions really "Through The Eyes Of One?"

Kevin Hines

Follow me on facebook at:
www.facebook.com/throughtheeyesofone

Through the Eyes of One?

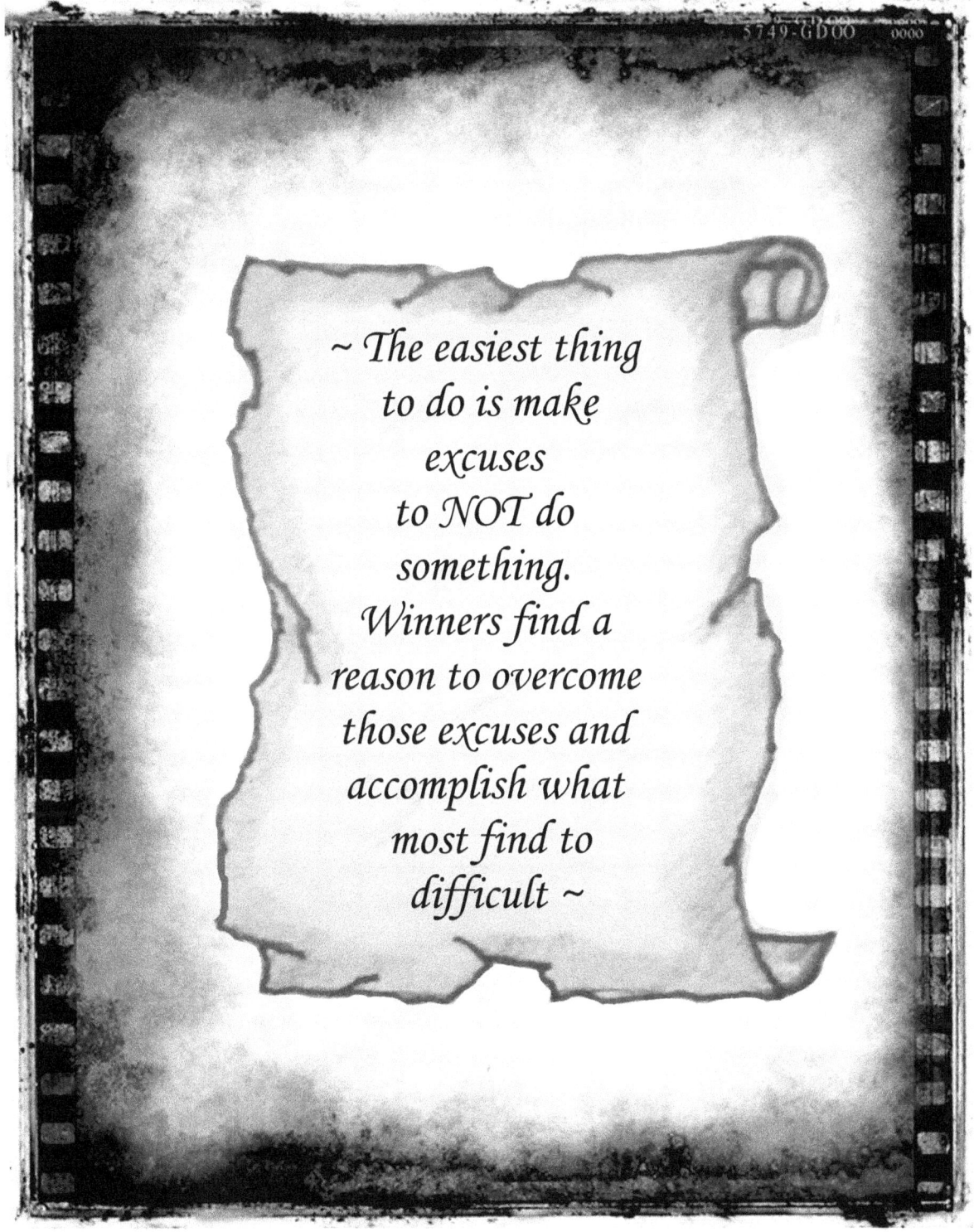

~ The easiest thing to do is make excuses to NOT do something. Winners find a reason to overcome those excuses and accomplish what most find to difficult ~

Through The Eyes Of One?

Your Thoughts

~ Being truly honest
with yourself is
extremely difficult
but you will be
a prisoner of
your own lies
until
you are ~

Your Thoughts

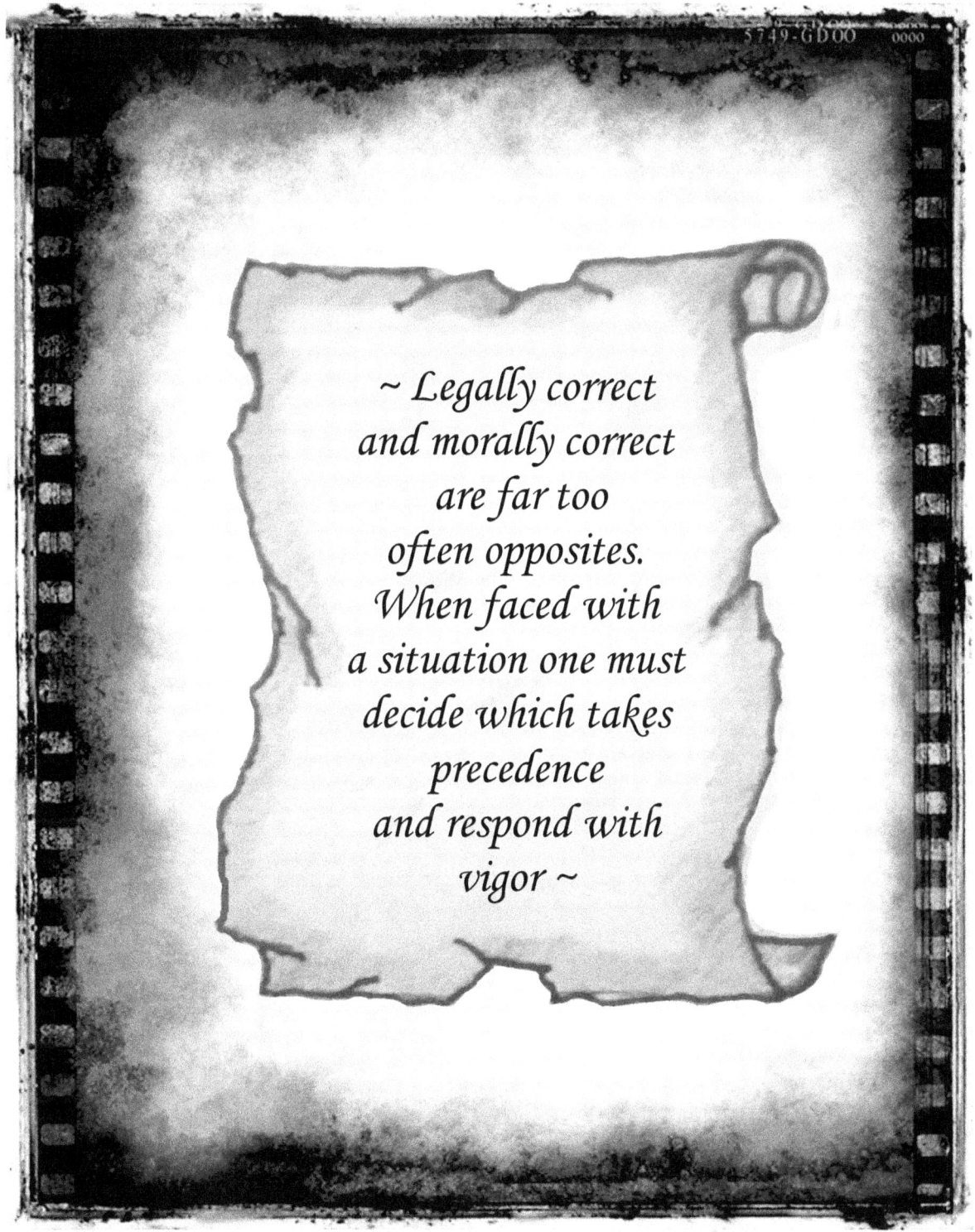

~ Legally correct
and morally correct
are far too
often opposites.
When faced with
a situation one must
decide which takes
precedence
and respond with
vigor ~

Your Thoughts

~ Money has a way of compromising peoples integrity ~

Your Thoughts

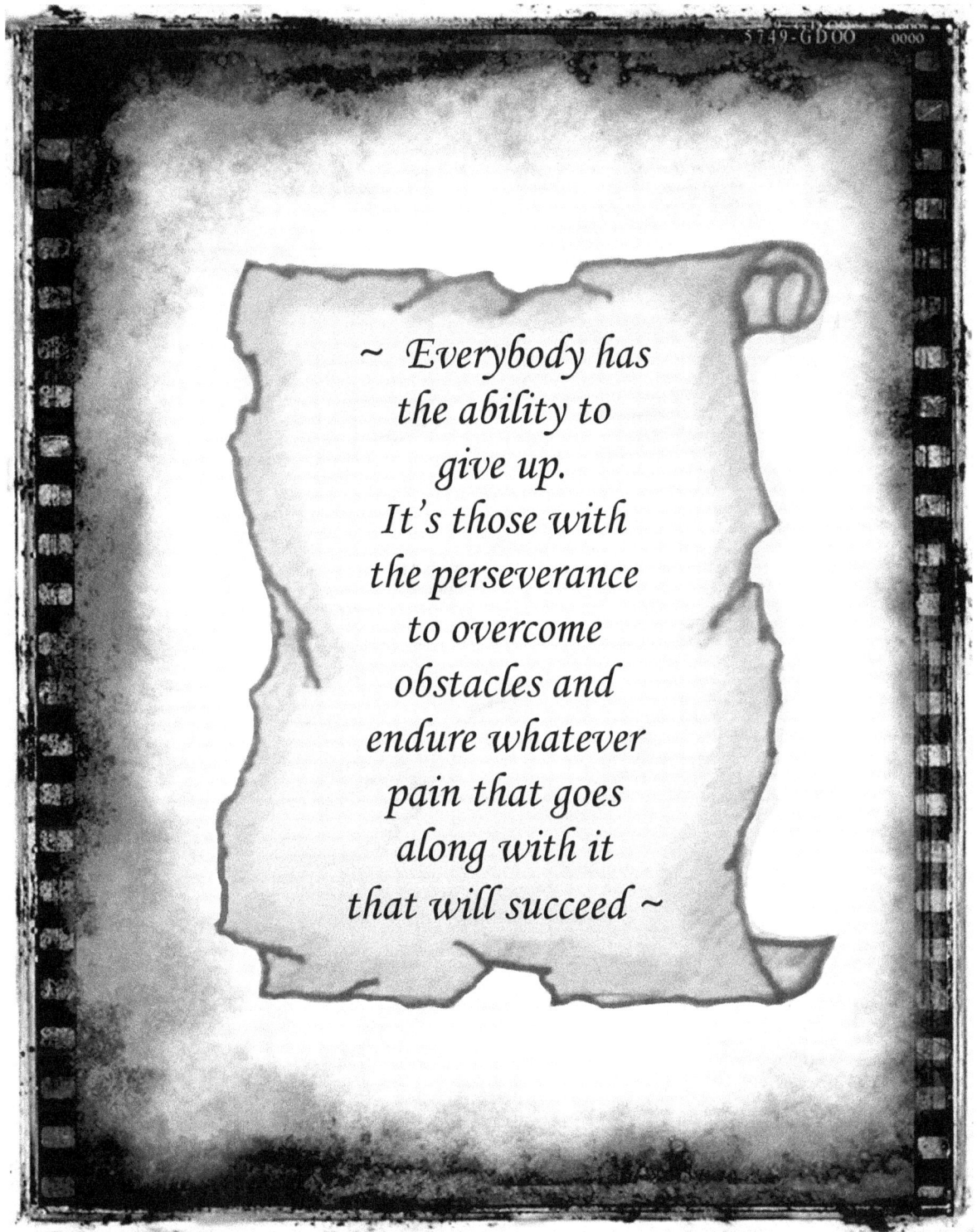

~ Everybody has the ability to give up. It's those with the perseverance to overcome obstacles and endure whatever pain that goes along with it that will succeed ~

Your Thoughts

~ Do everything from your heart and if your heart is pure you will never be wrong ~

Your Thoughts

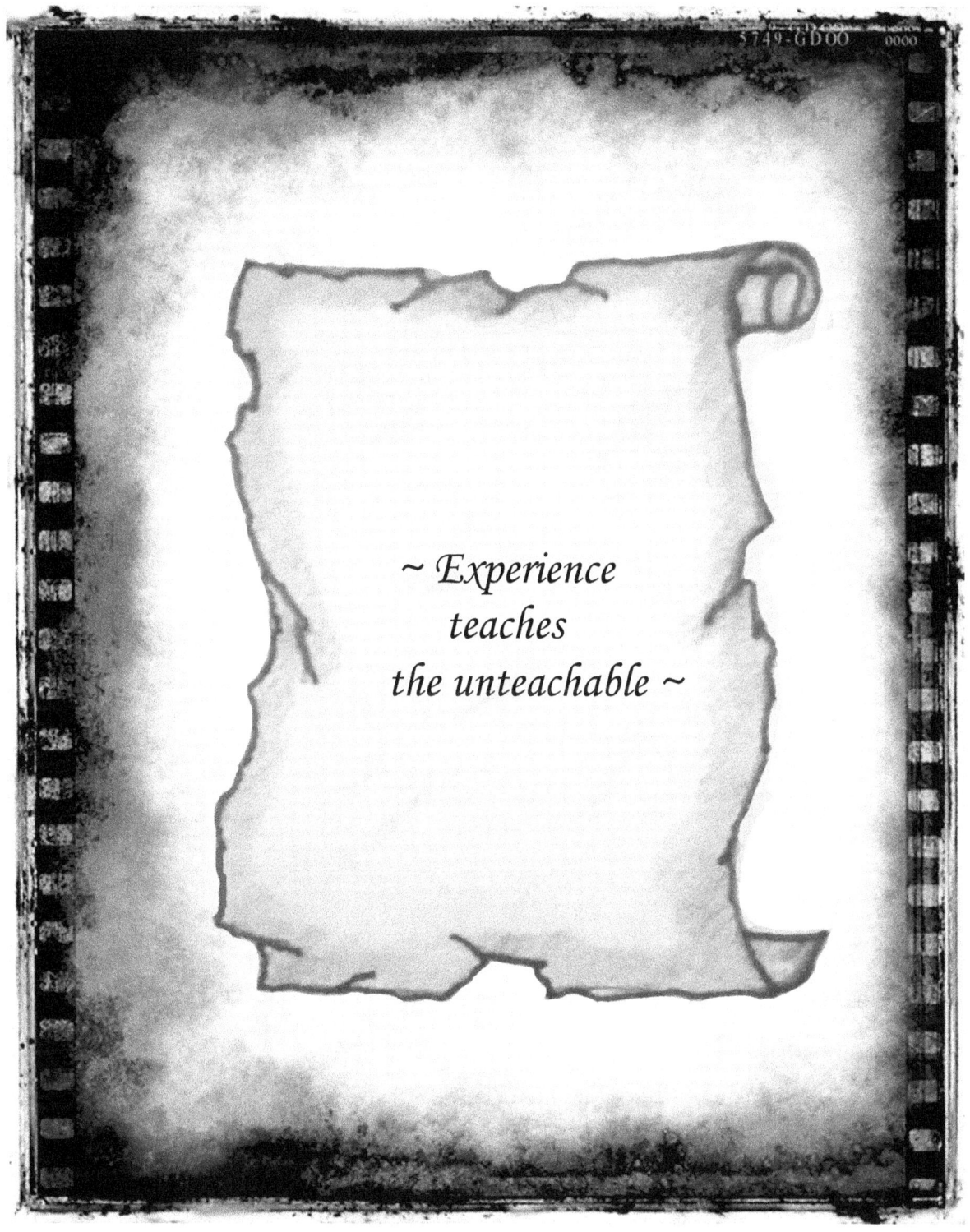

~ Experience
teaches
the unteachable ~

Your Thoughts

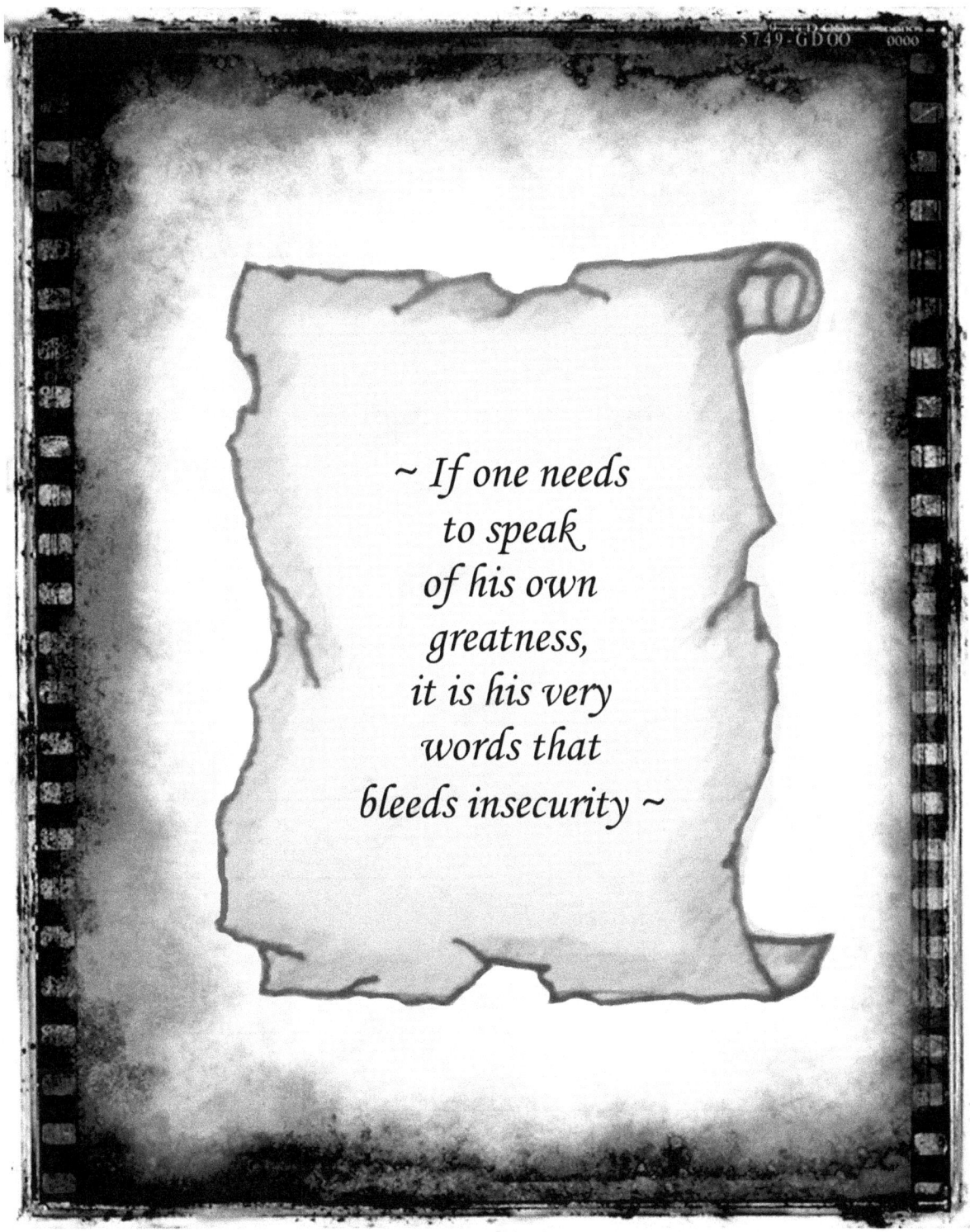

~ If one needs to speak of his own greatness, it is his very words that bleeds insecurity ~

Your Thoughts

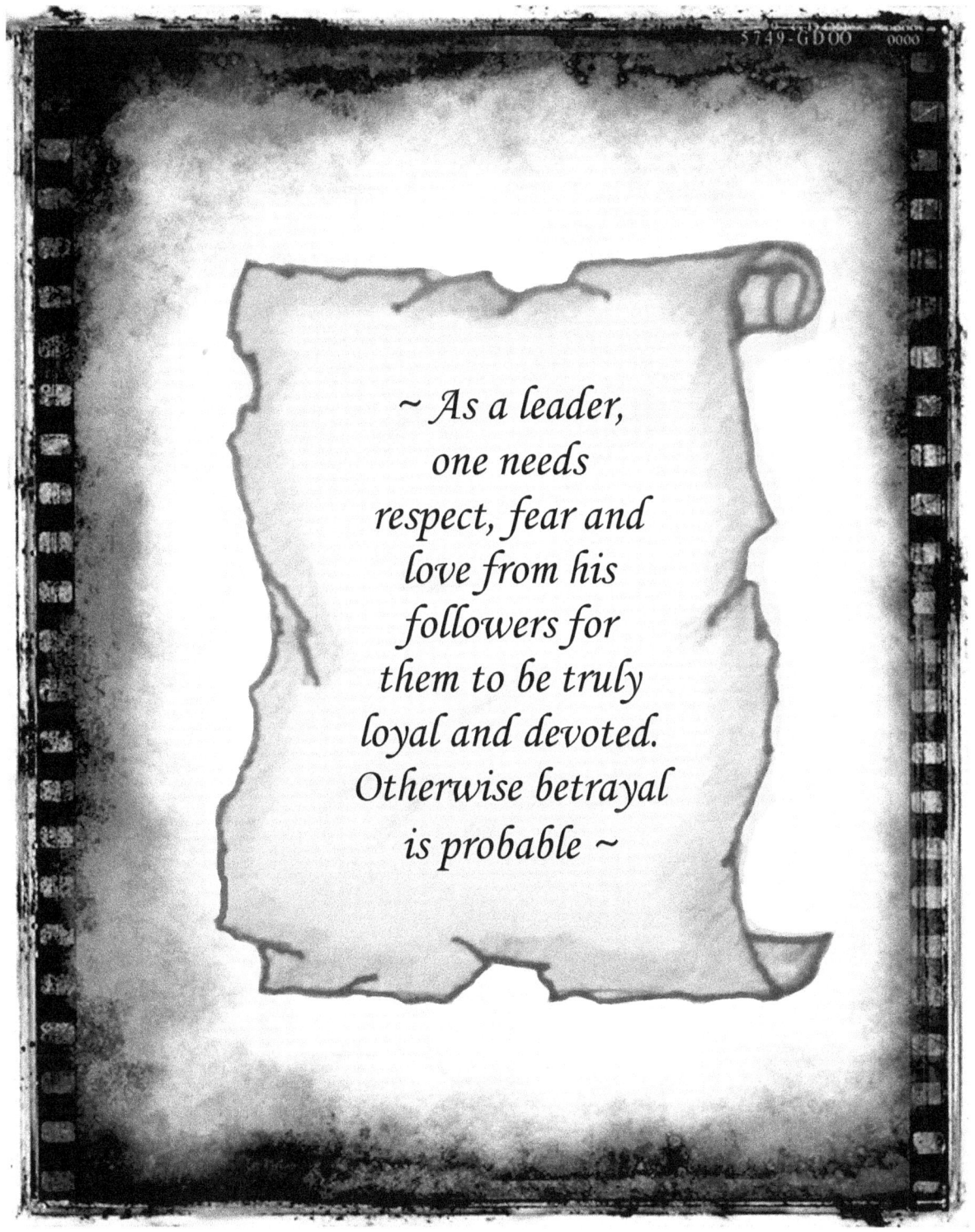

~ As a leader, one needs respect, fear and love from his followers for them to be truly loyal and devoted. Otherwise betrayal is probable ~

Your Thoughts

~ *Contentment is the kiss of death* ~

Your Thoughts

~ To be an effective leader,
one must be
an effective listener ~

Your Thoughts

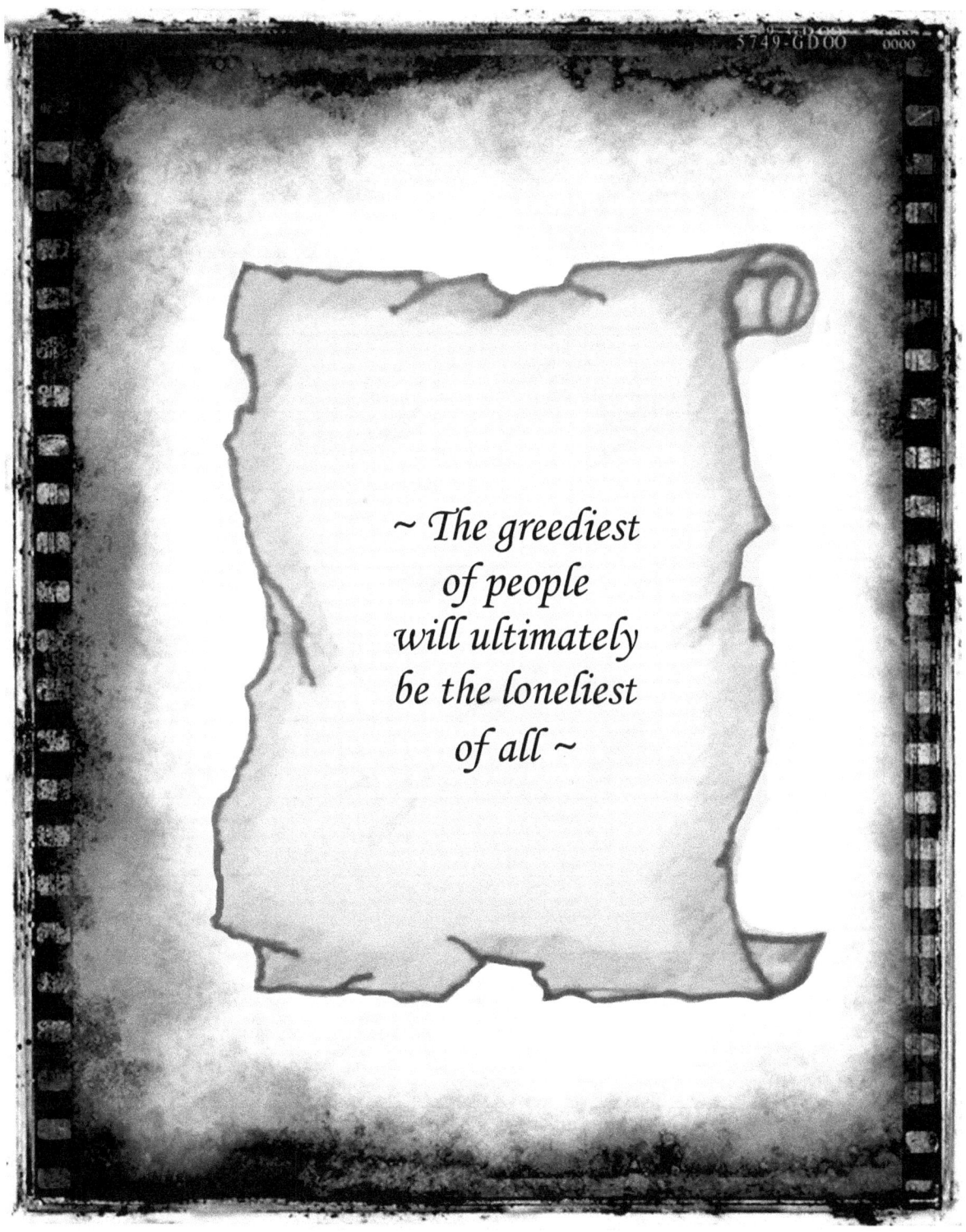

~ The greediest of people will ultimately be the loneliest of all ~

Your Thoughts

*~ Jealousy is
a clear window
for all to see
ones insecurities ~*

Your Thoughts

~ *Stand alone and you will always be king* ~

Your Thoughts

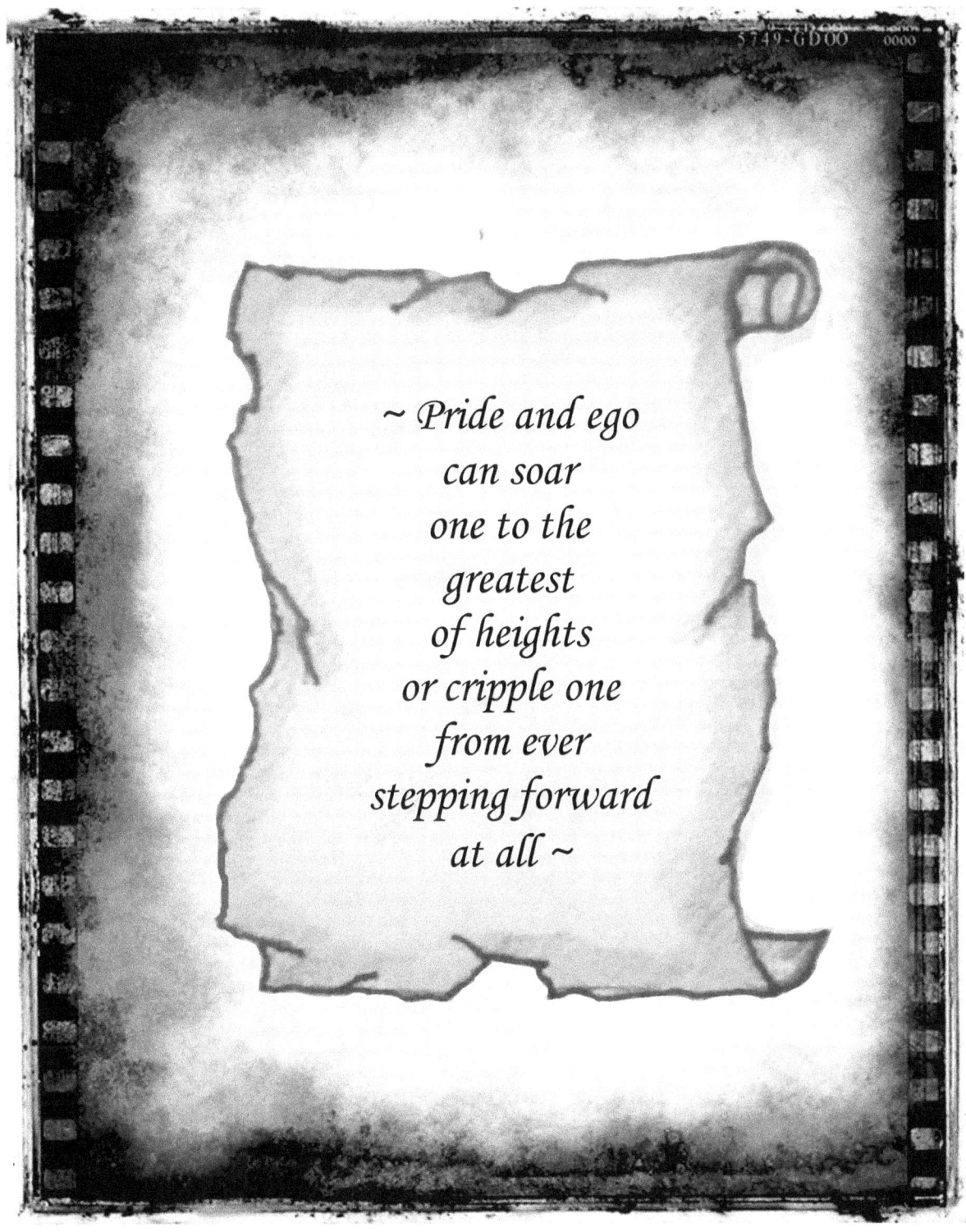

~ Pride and ego
can soar
one to the
greatest
of heights
or cripple one
from ever
stepping forward
at all ~

Your Thoughts

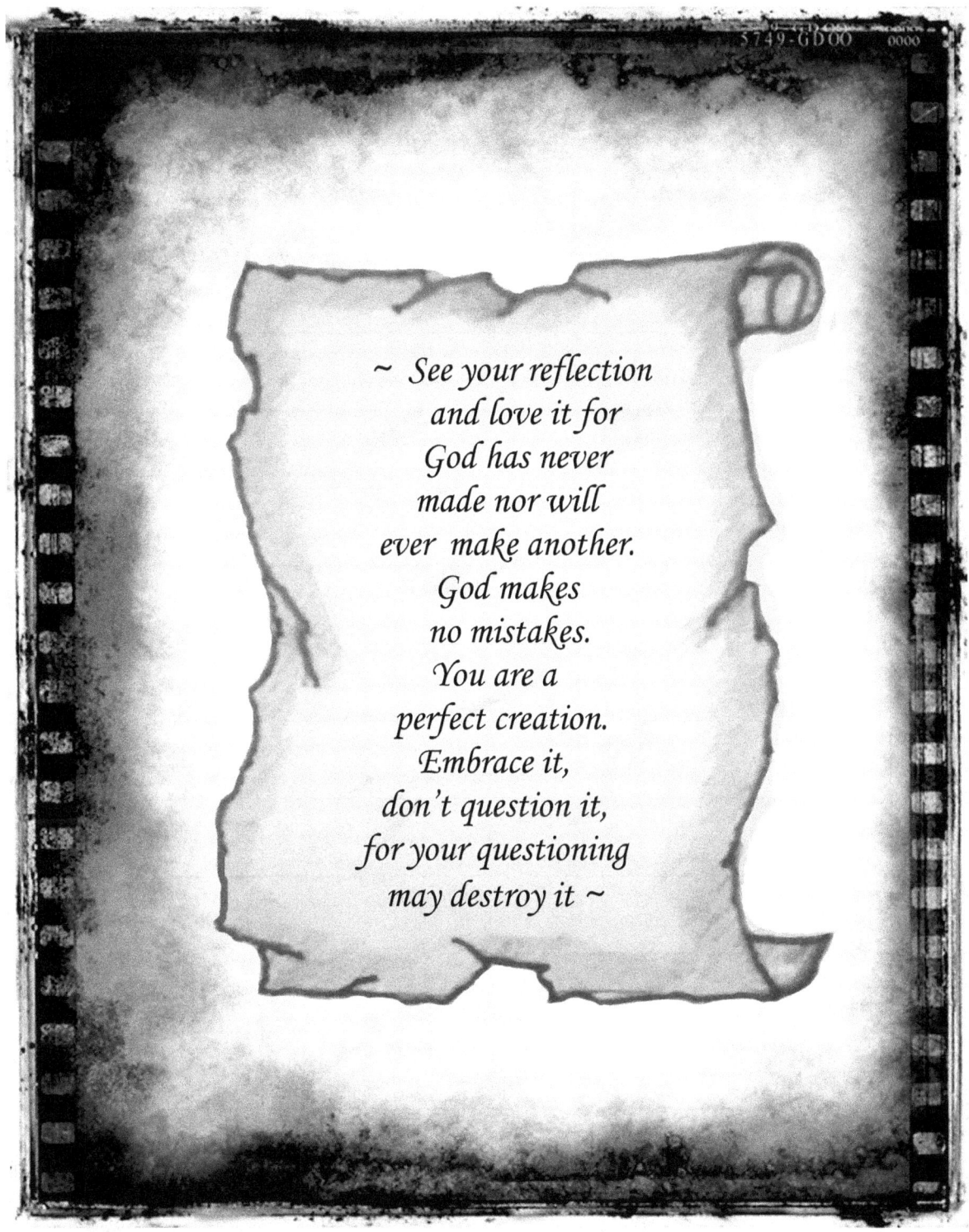

~ See your reflection
and love it for
God has never
made nor will
ever make another.
God makes
no mistakes.
You are a
perfect creation.
Embrace it,
don't question it,
for your questioning
may destroy it ~

Your Thoughts

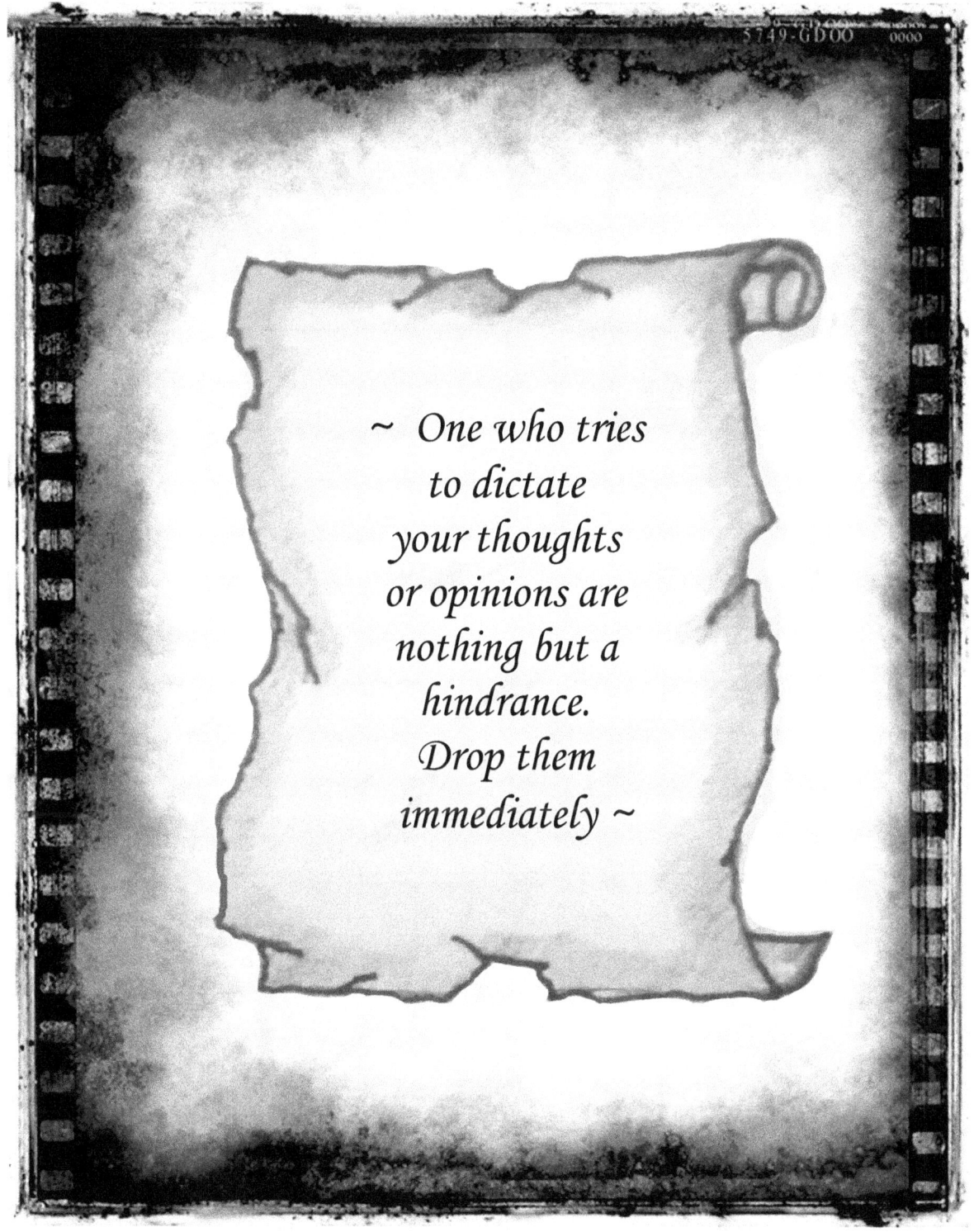

Your Thoughts

~ Evil does not introduce itself as evil, it comes incognito ~

Your Thoughts

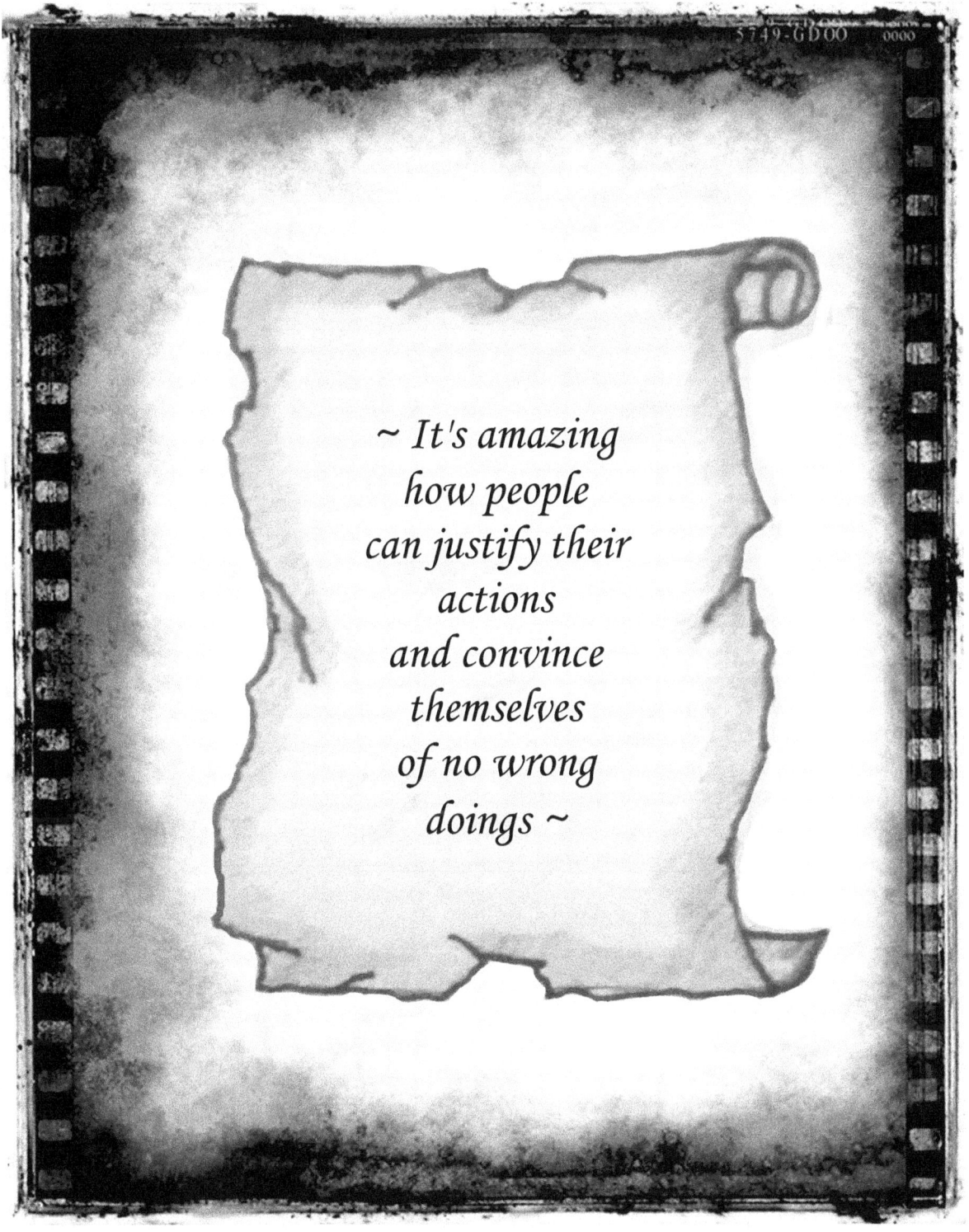

~ It's amazing how people can justify their actions and convince themselves of no wrong doings ~

Your Thoughts

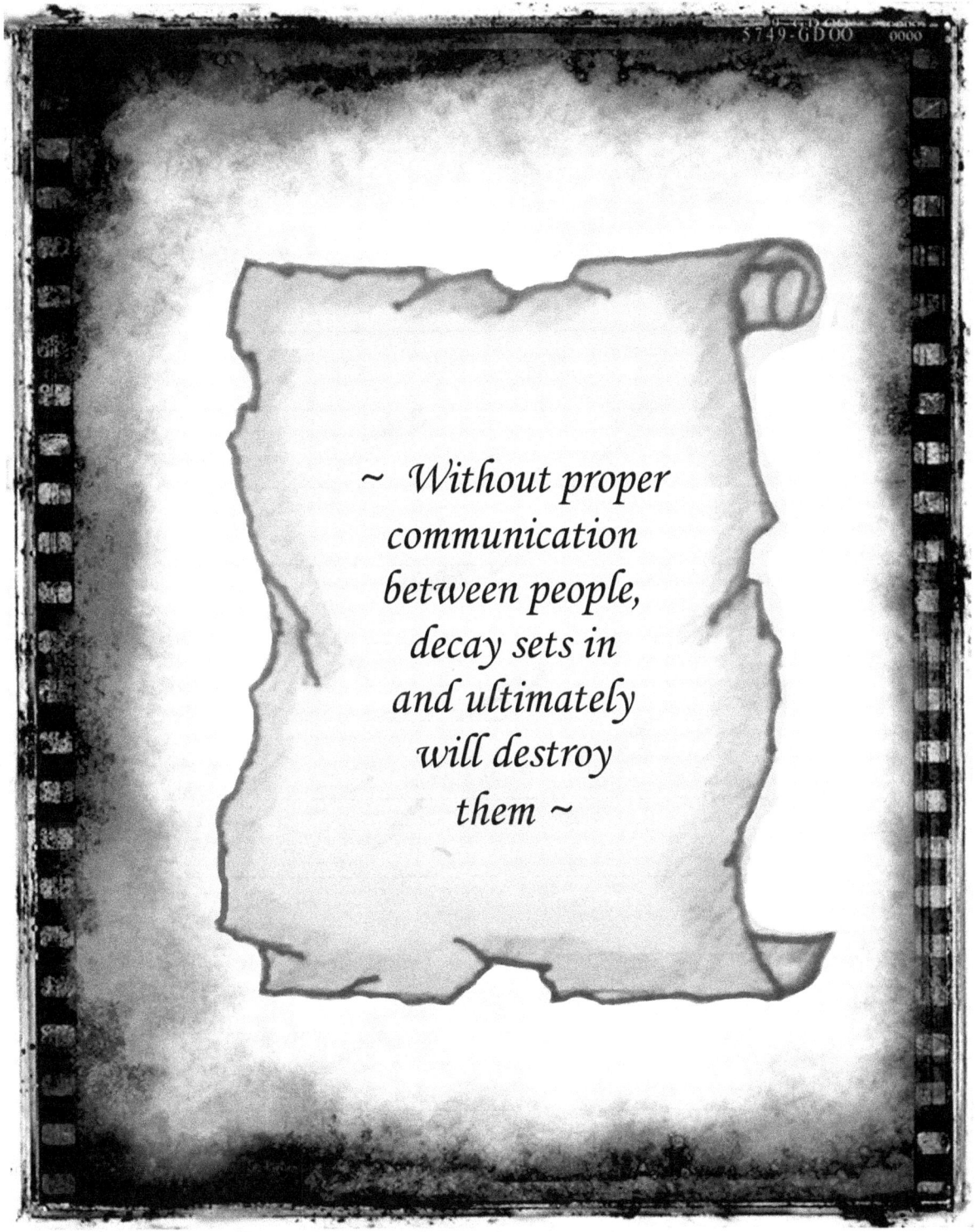

~ *Without proper communication between people, decay sets in and ultimately will destroy them* ~

Your Thoughts

~ Making the right decision often leaves one extremely lonely ~

Your Thoughts

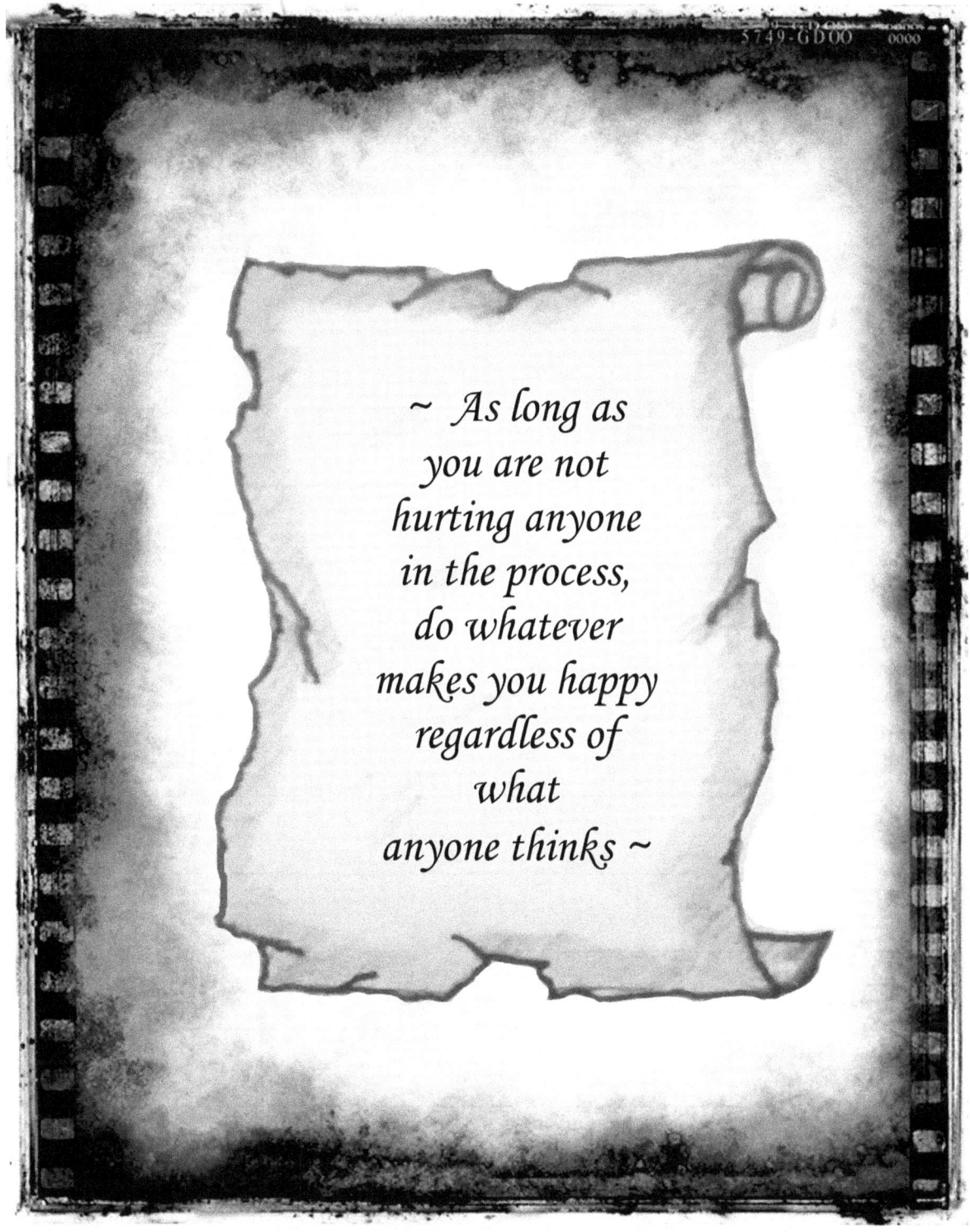

~ As long as you are not hurting anyone in the process, do whatever makes you happy regardless of what anyone thinks ~

Your Thoughts

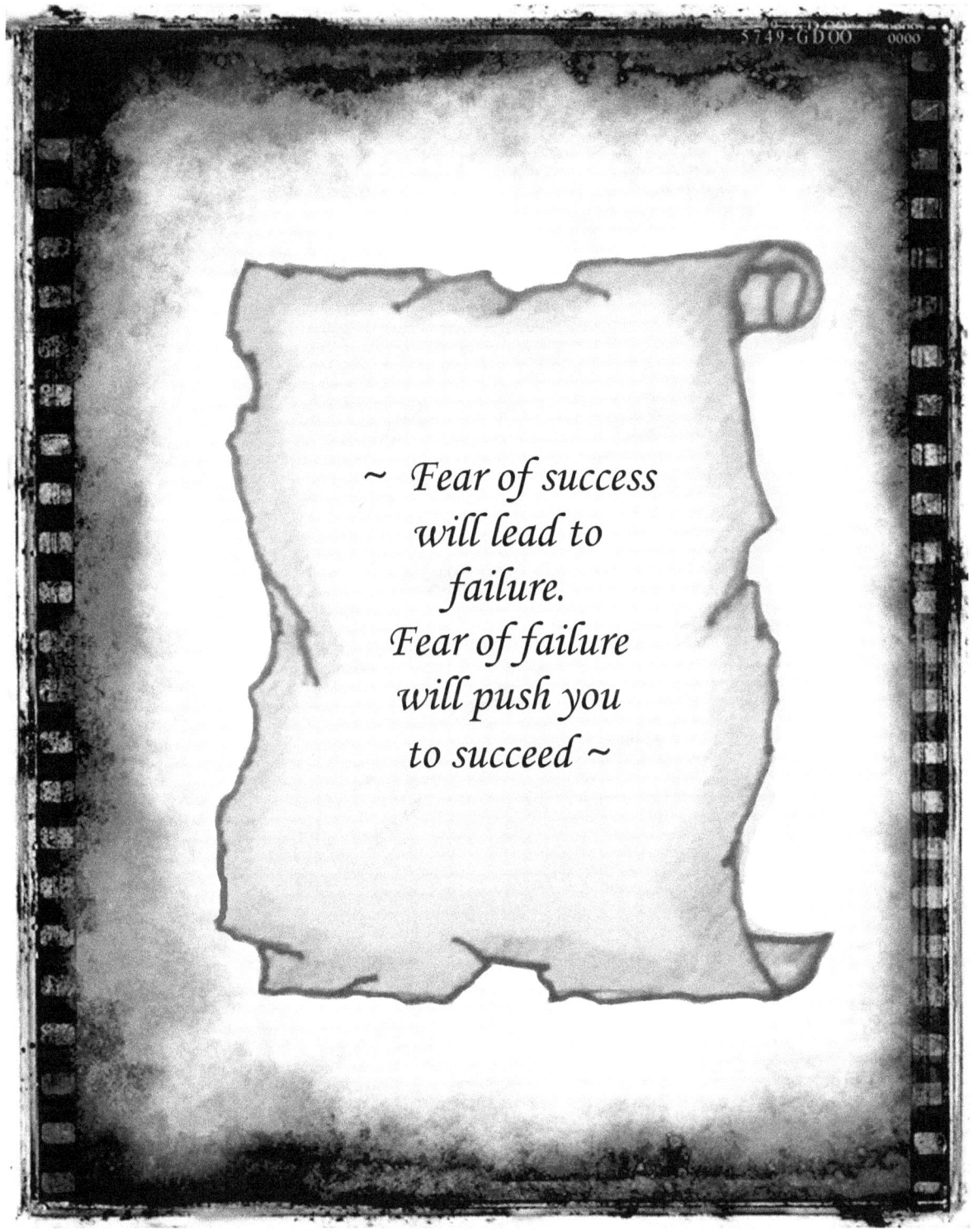

~ *Fear of success will lead to failure. Fear of failure will push you to succeed* ~

Your Thoughts

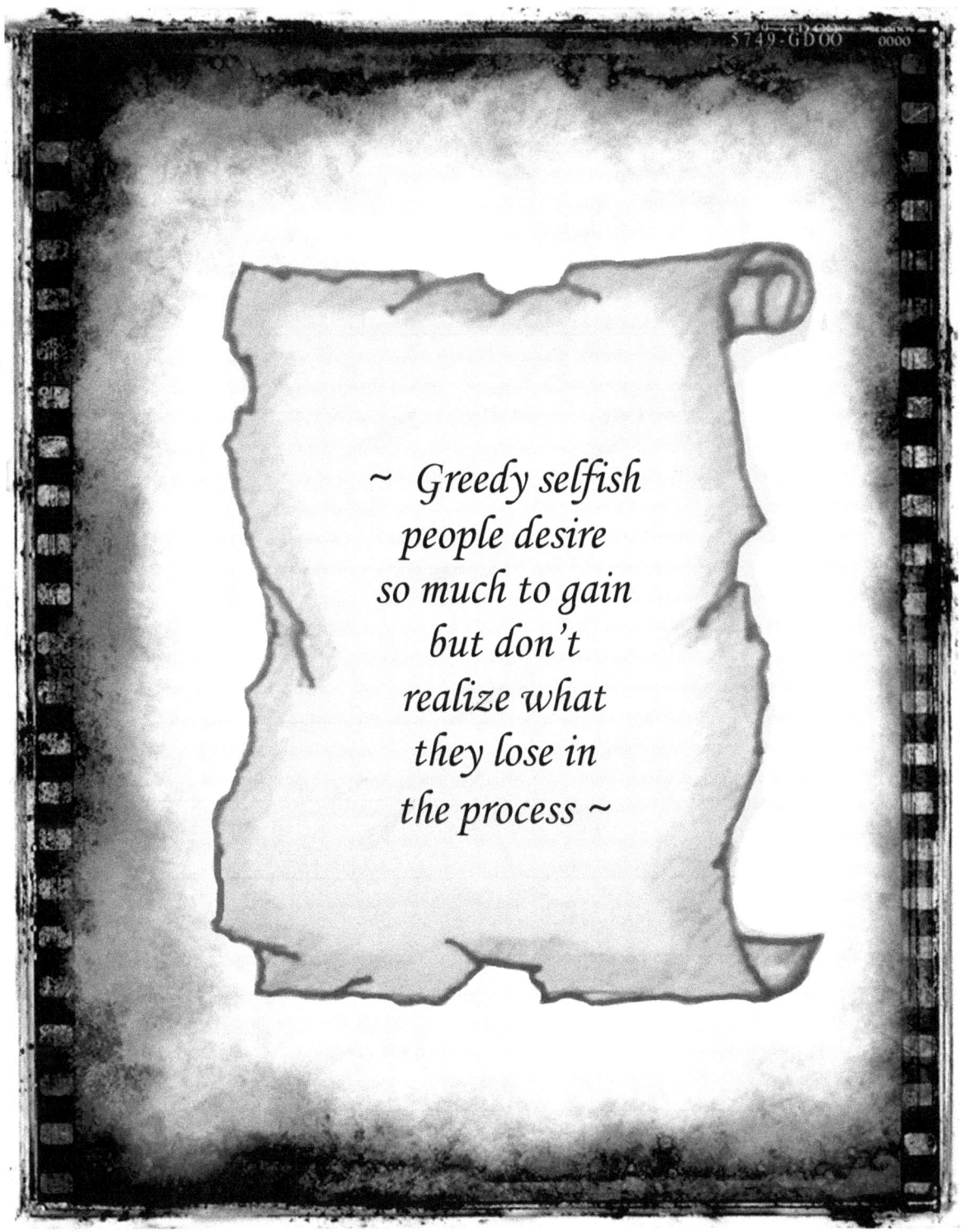

~ Greedy selfish people desire so much to gain but don't realize what they lose in the process ~

Your Thoughts

~ When one
quits
they never even
give themselves
the opportunity
to succeed ~

Your Thoughts

~ *Negativity is contagious* ~

Your Thoughts

Your Thoughts

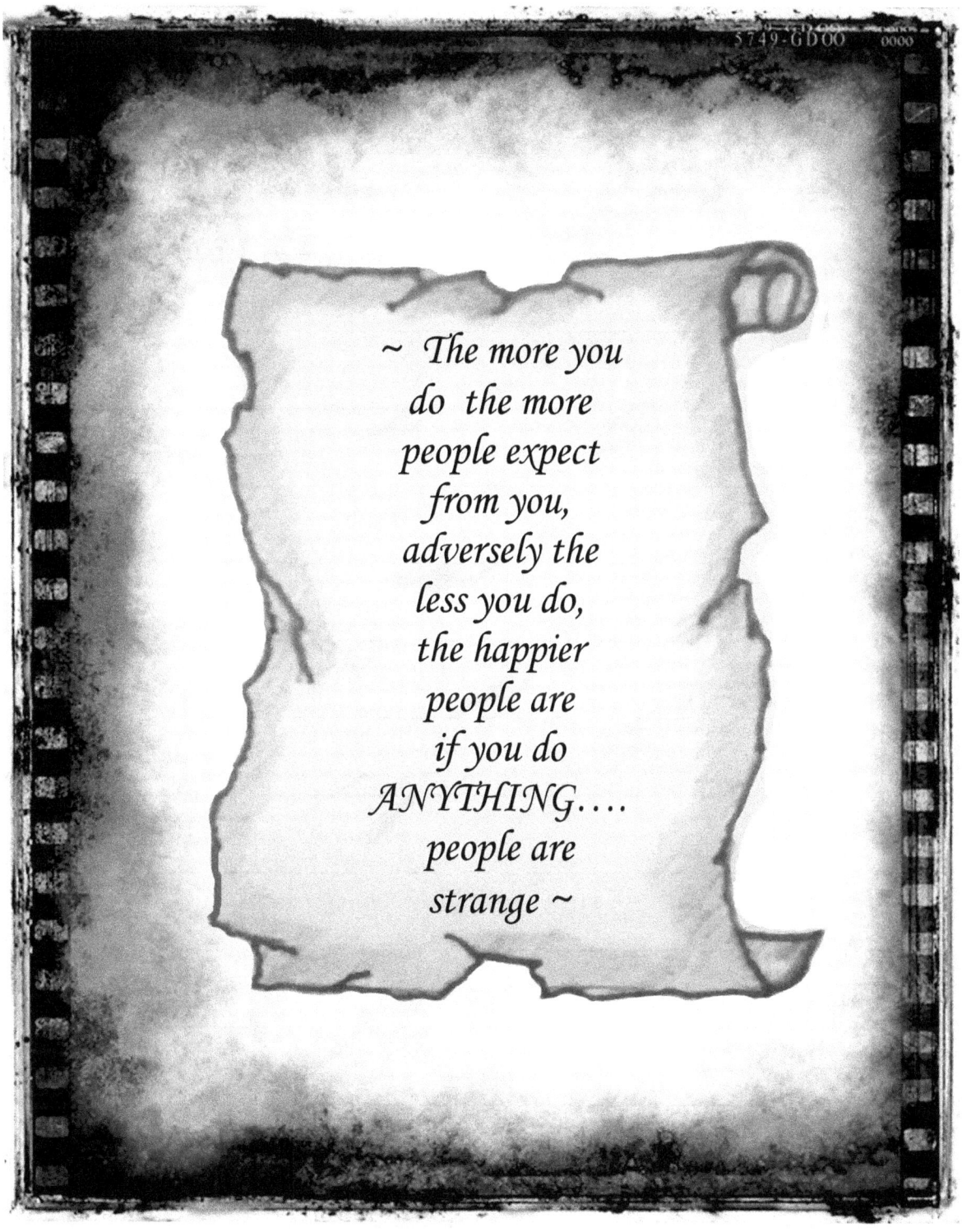

~ The more you do the more people expect from you, adversely the less you do, the happier people are if you do ANYTHING.... people are strange ~

Your Thoughts

~ Those who live without passion for something are merely existing ~

Your Thoughts

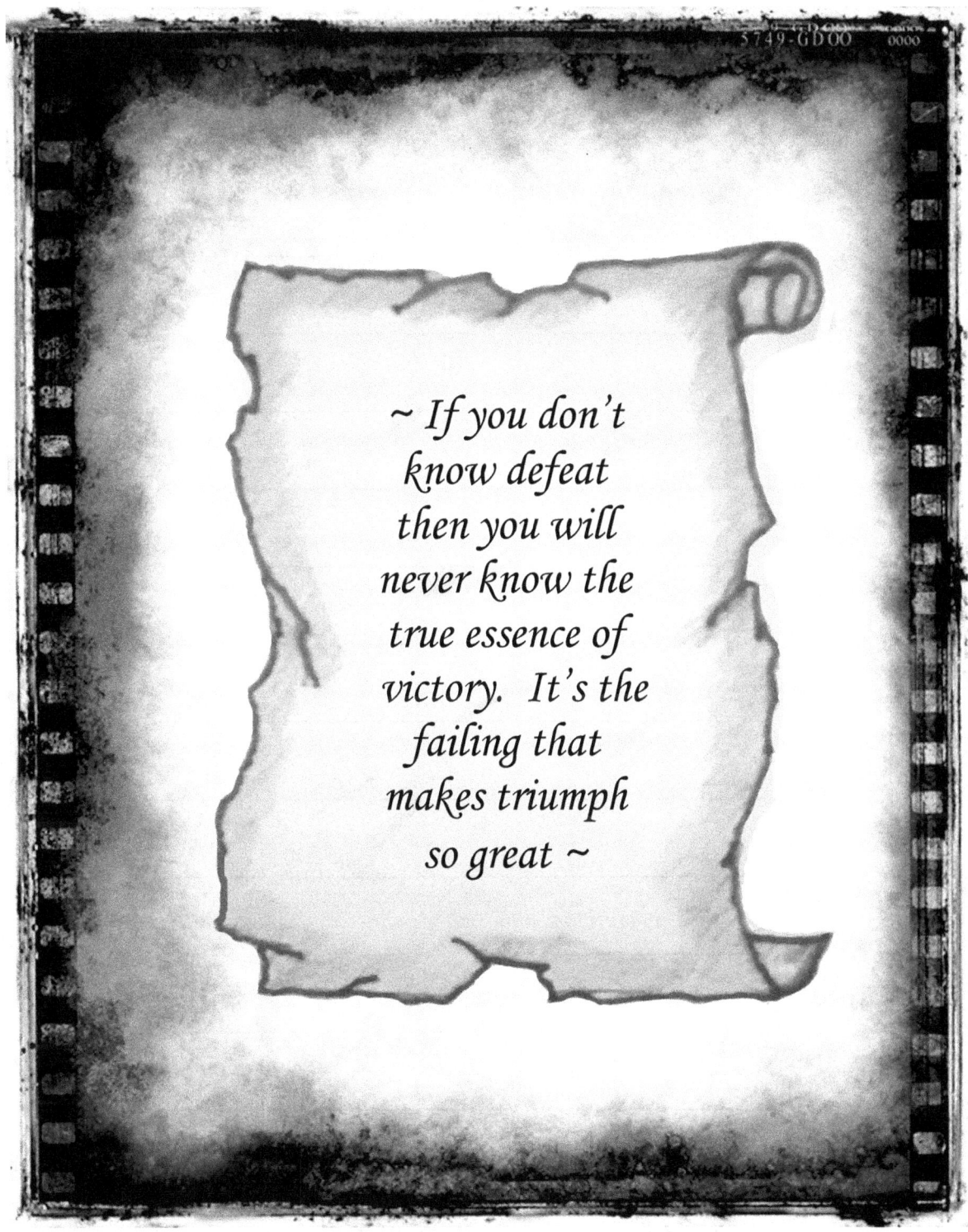

~ If you don't know defeat then you will never know the true essence of victory. It's the failing that makes triumph so great ~

Your Thoughts

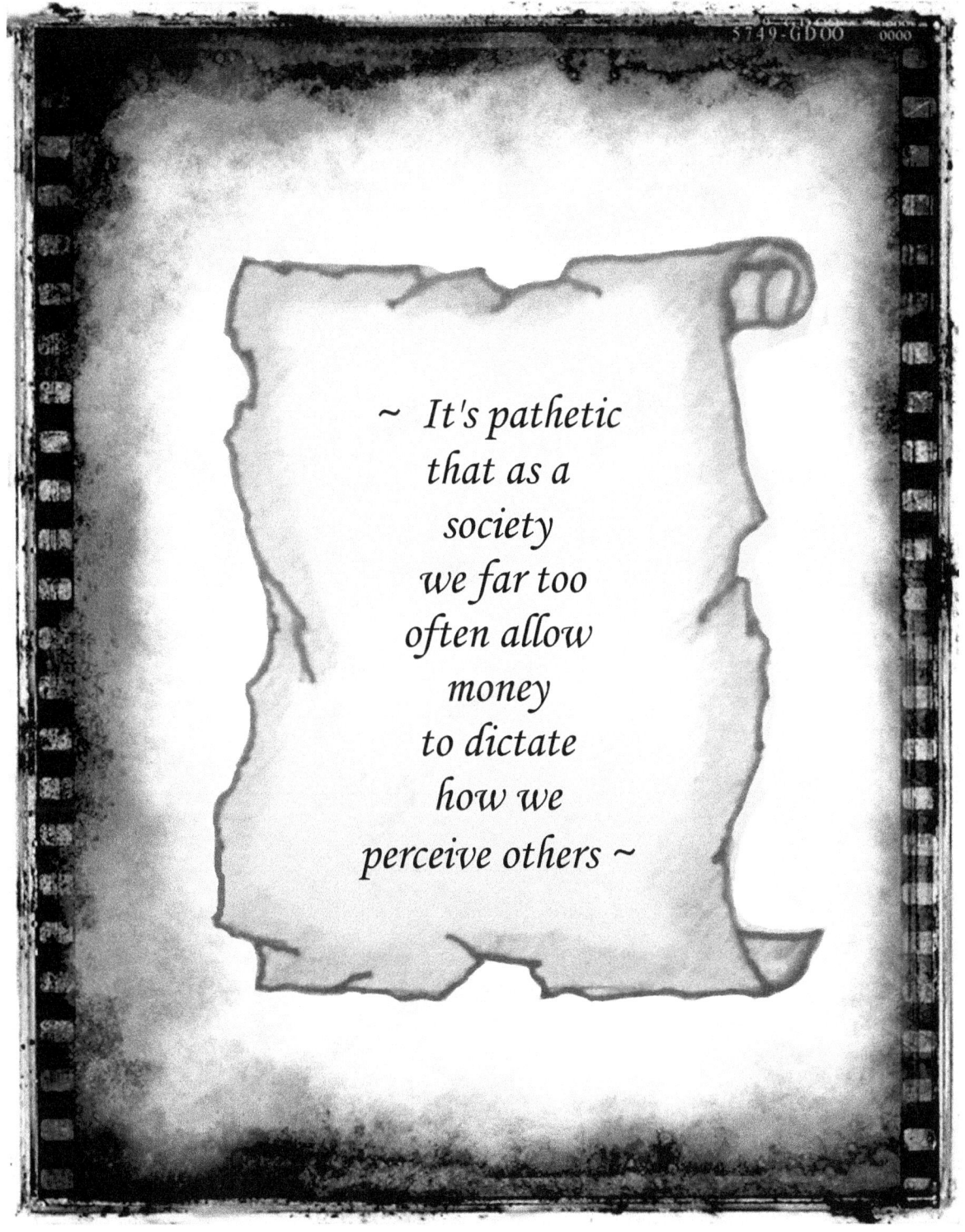

~ It's pathetic that as a society we far too often allow money to dictate how we perceive others ~

Your Thoughts

~ Make no waves where there is no water ~

Your Thoughts

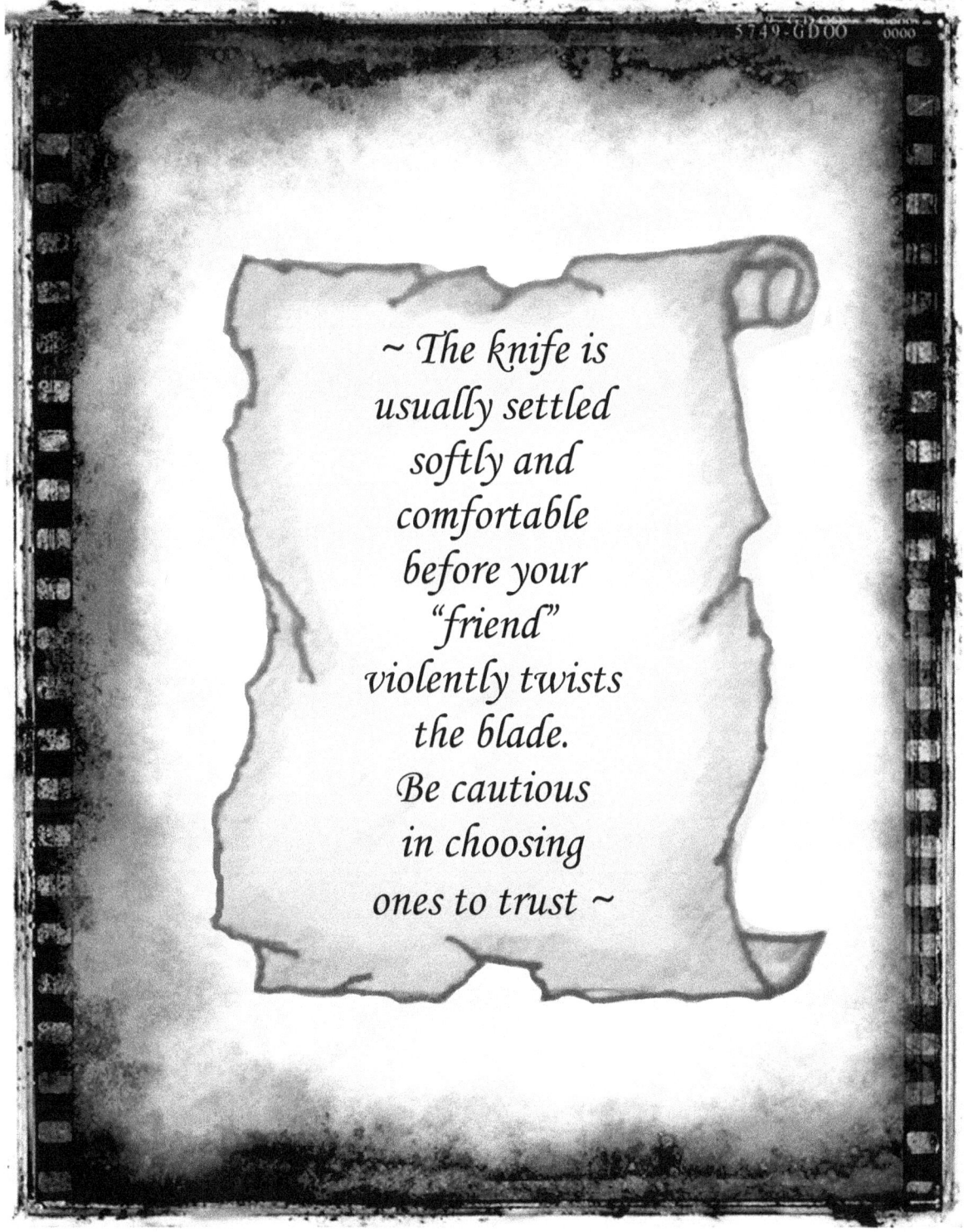

~ The knife is usually settled softly and comfortable before your "friend" violently twists the blade. Be cautious in choosing ones to trust ~

Your Thoughts

~ The first step is usually the hardest ~

Your Thoughts

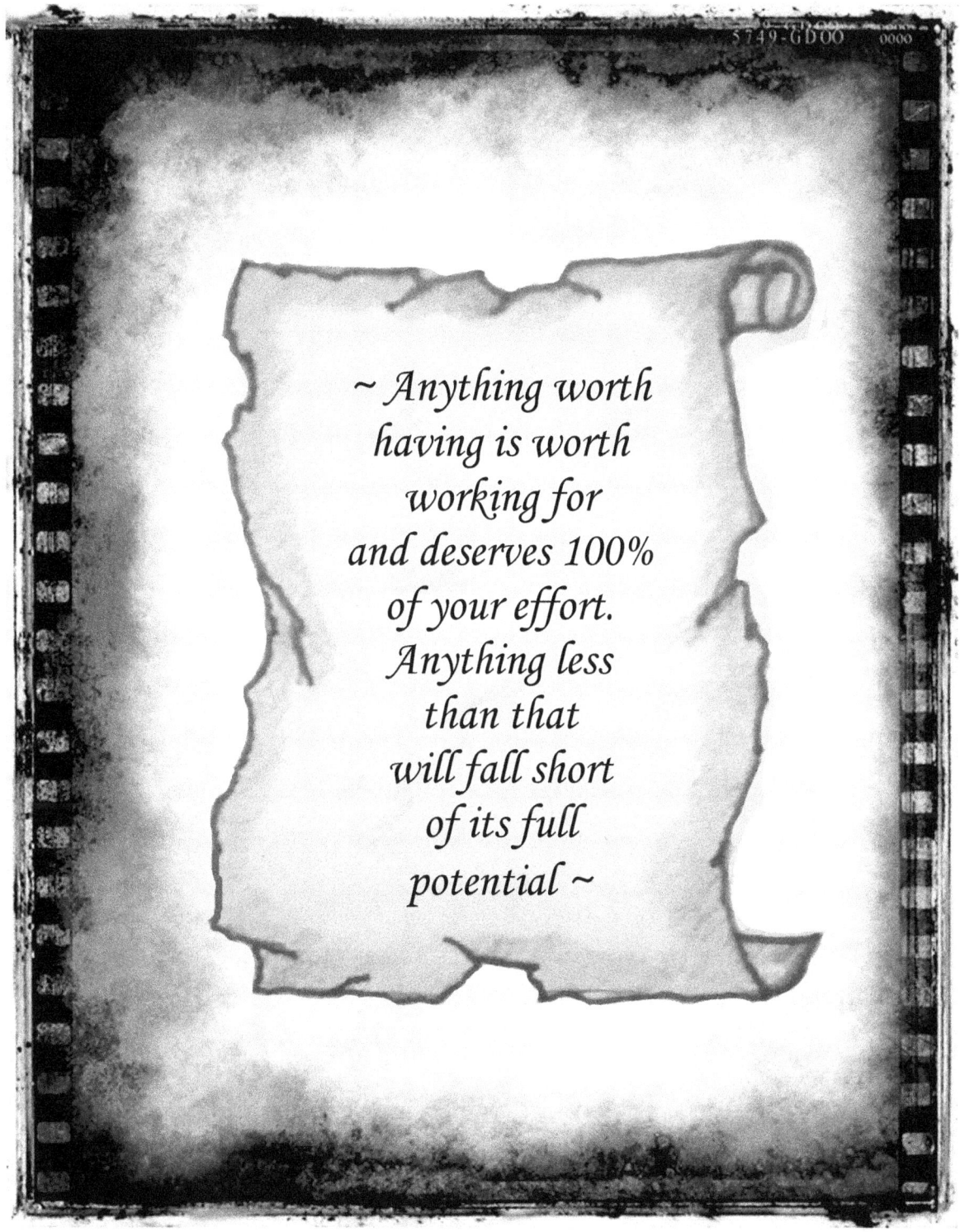

~ Anything worth having is worth working for and deserves 100% of your effort. Anything less than that will fall short of its full potential ~

Your Thoughts

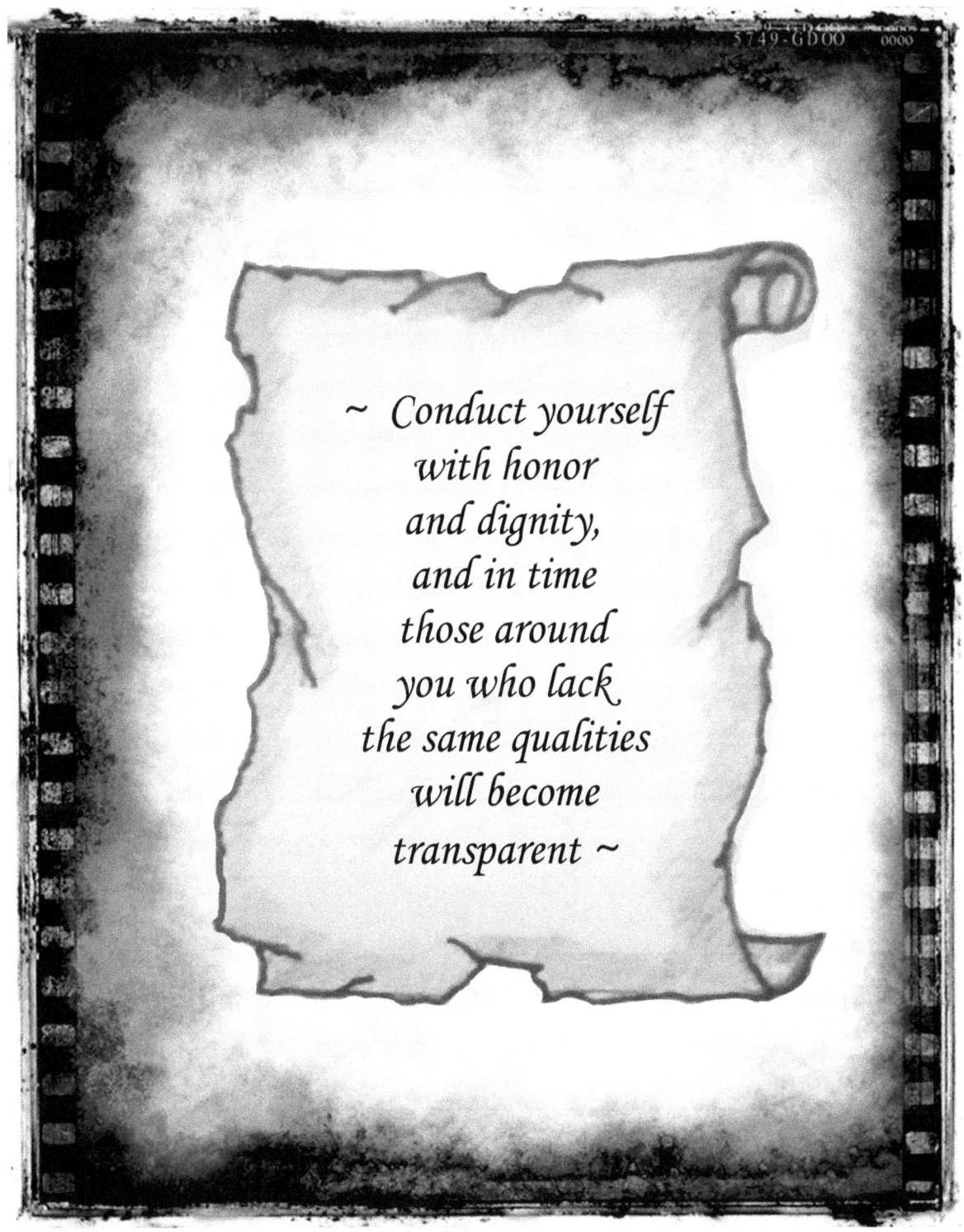

~ Conduct yourself with honor and dignity, and in time those around you who lack the same qualities will become transparent ~

Your Thoughts

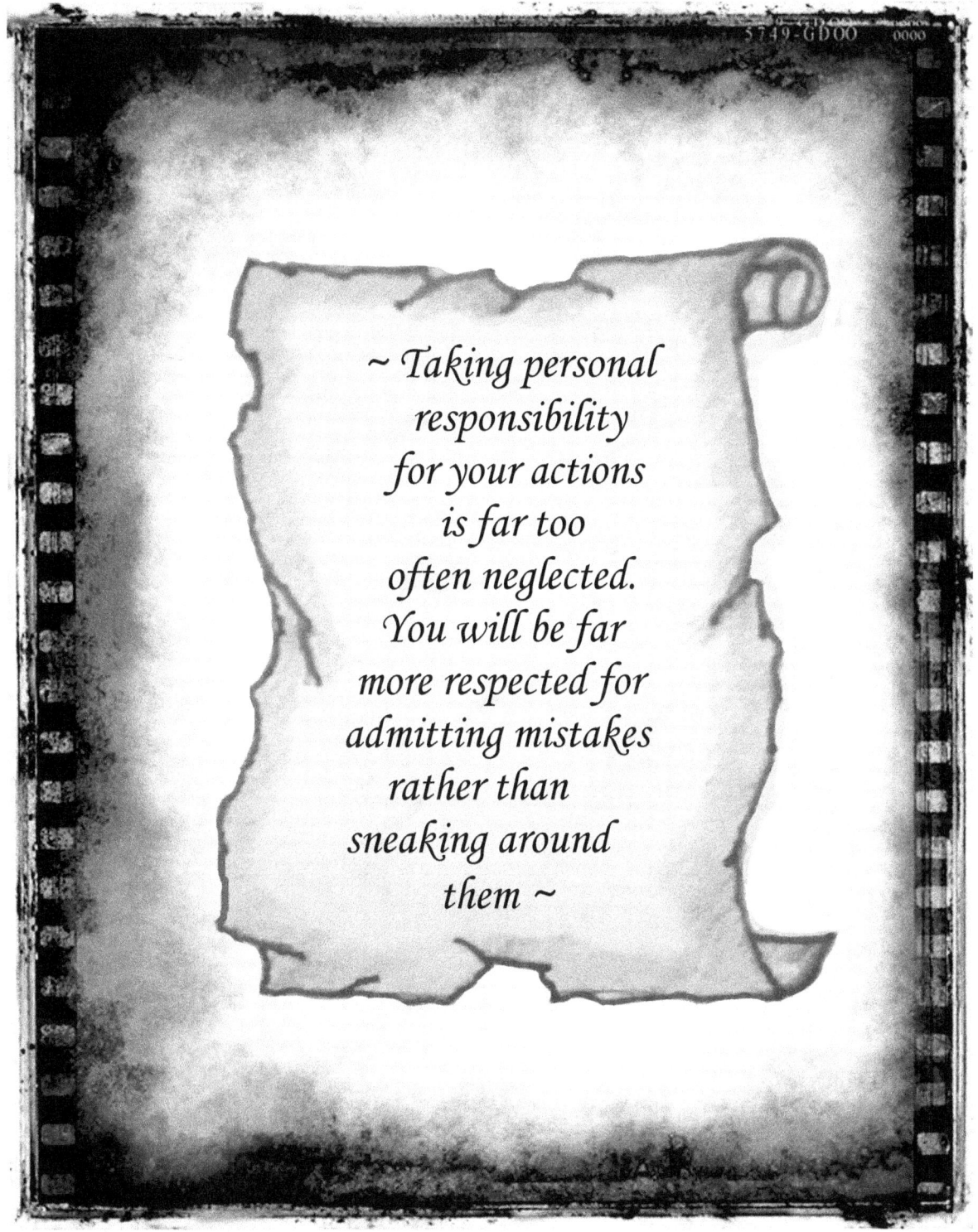

~ Taking personal responsibility for your actions is far too often neglected. You will be far more respected for admitting mistakes rather than sneaking around them ~

Your Thoughts

~ Positive attitude, positive energy and a positive mind breeds success. Don't let negative seep into your being ~

Your Thoughts

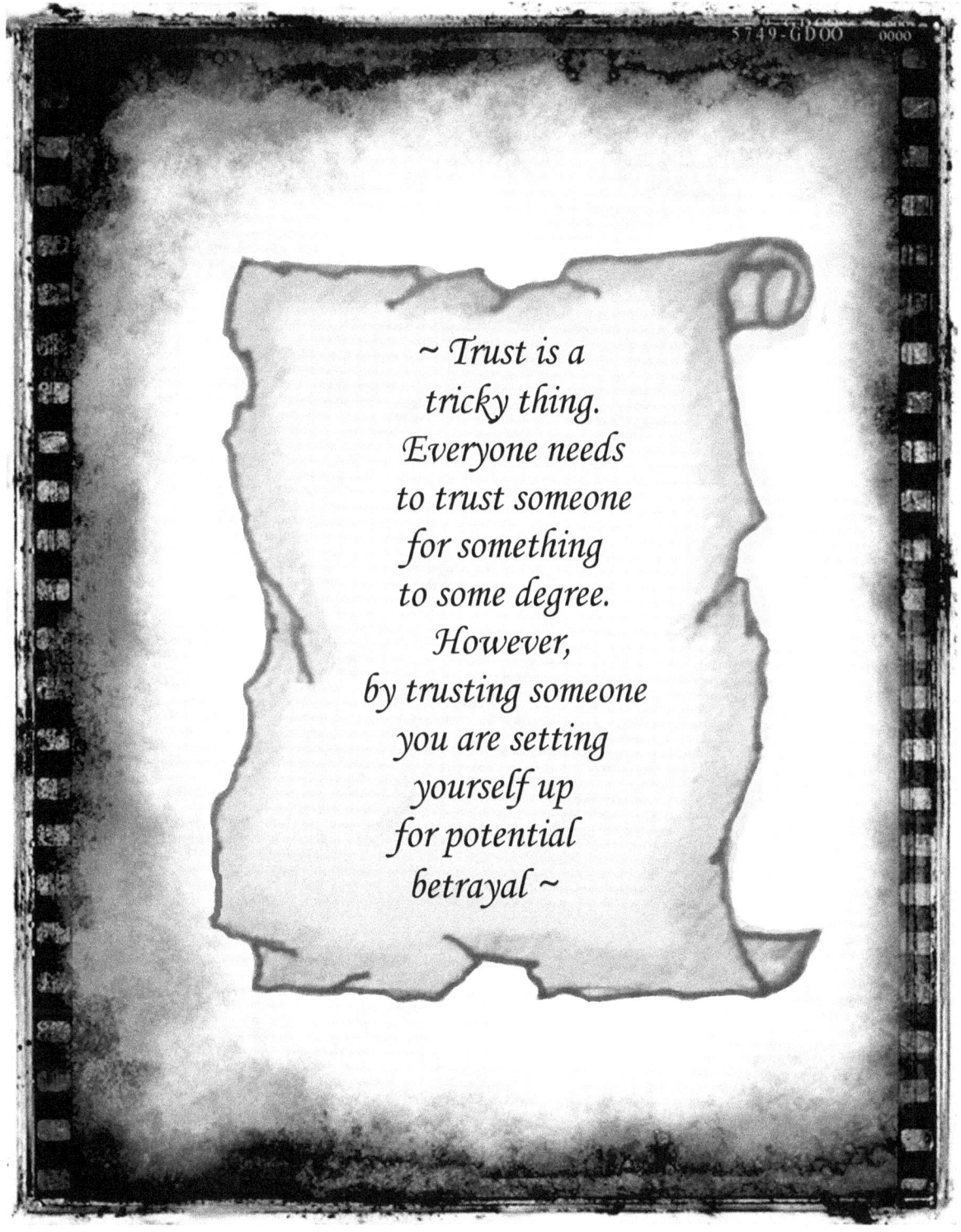

~ Trust is a tricky thing. Everyone needs to trust someone for something to some degree. However, by trusting someone you are setting yourself up for potential betrayal ~

Your Thoughts

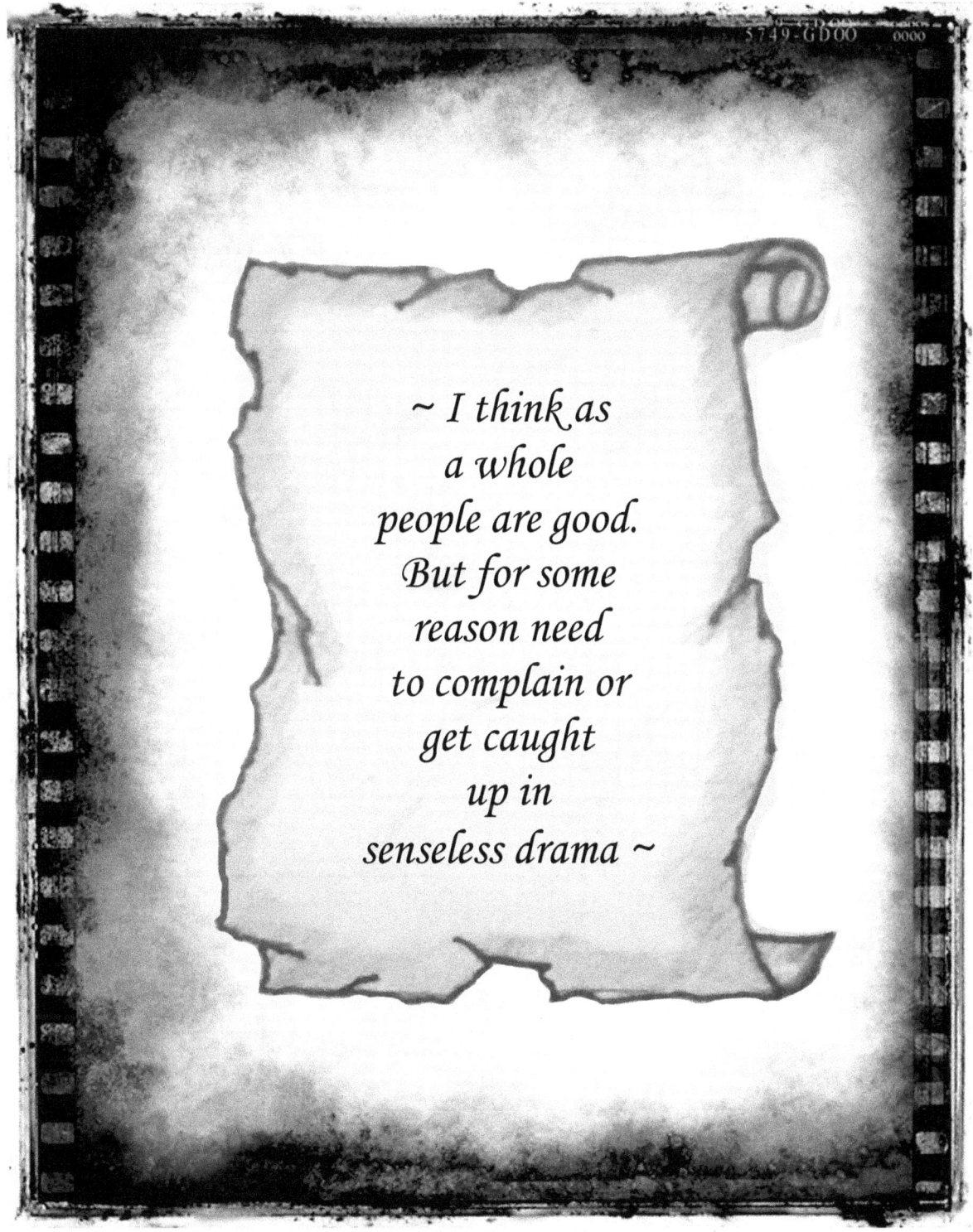

~ I think as
a whole
people are good.
But for some
reason need
to complain or
get caught
up in
senseless drama ~

Your Thoughts

~ A lot of times people stress needlessly. Take a step back and usually you will find it really doesn't matter at all ~

Your Thoughts

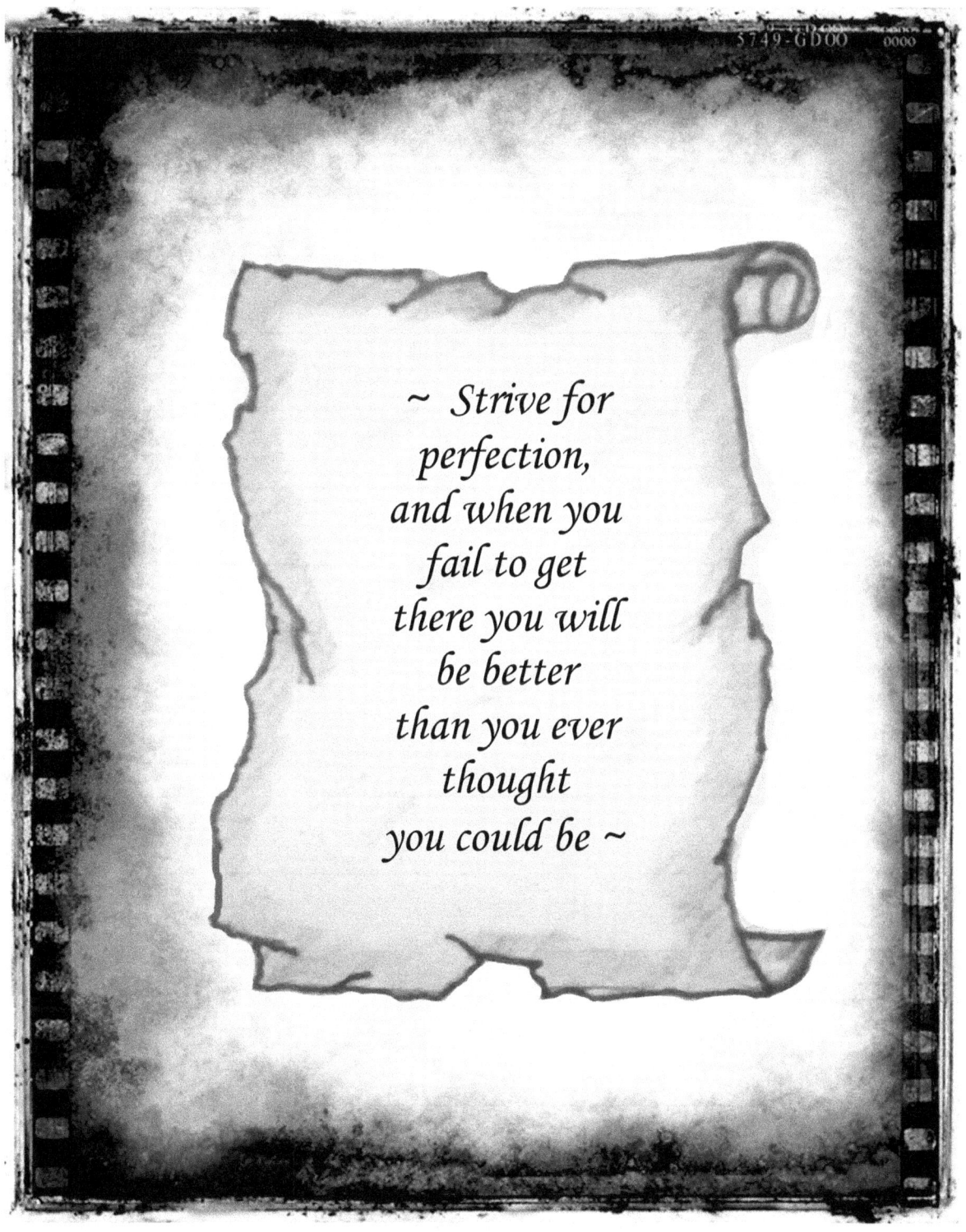

~ Strive for perfection, and when you fail to get there you will be better than you ever thought you could be ~

Your Thoughts

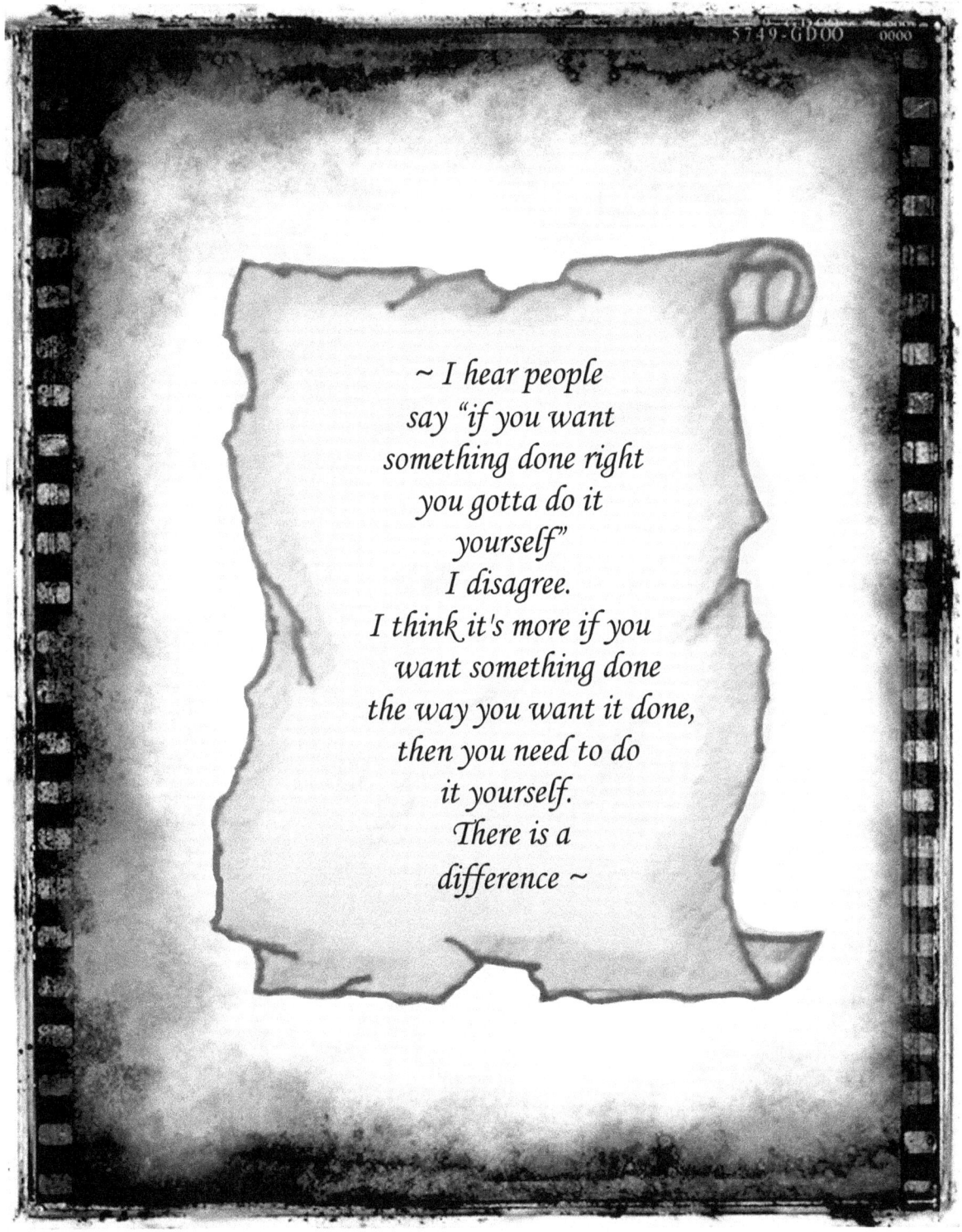

~ I hear people say "if you want something done right you gotta do it yourself"
I disagree.
I think it's more if you want something done the way you want it done, then you need to do it yourself.
There is a difference ~

Your Thoughts

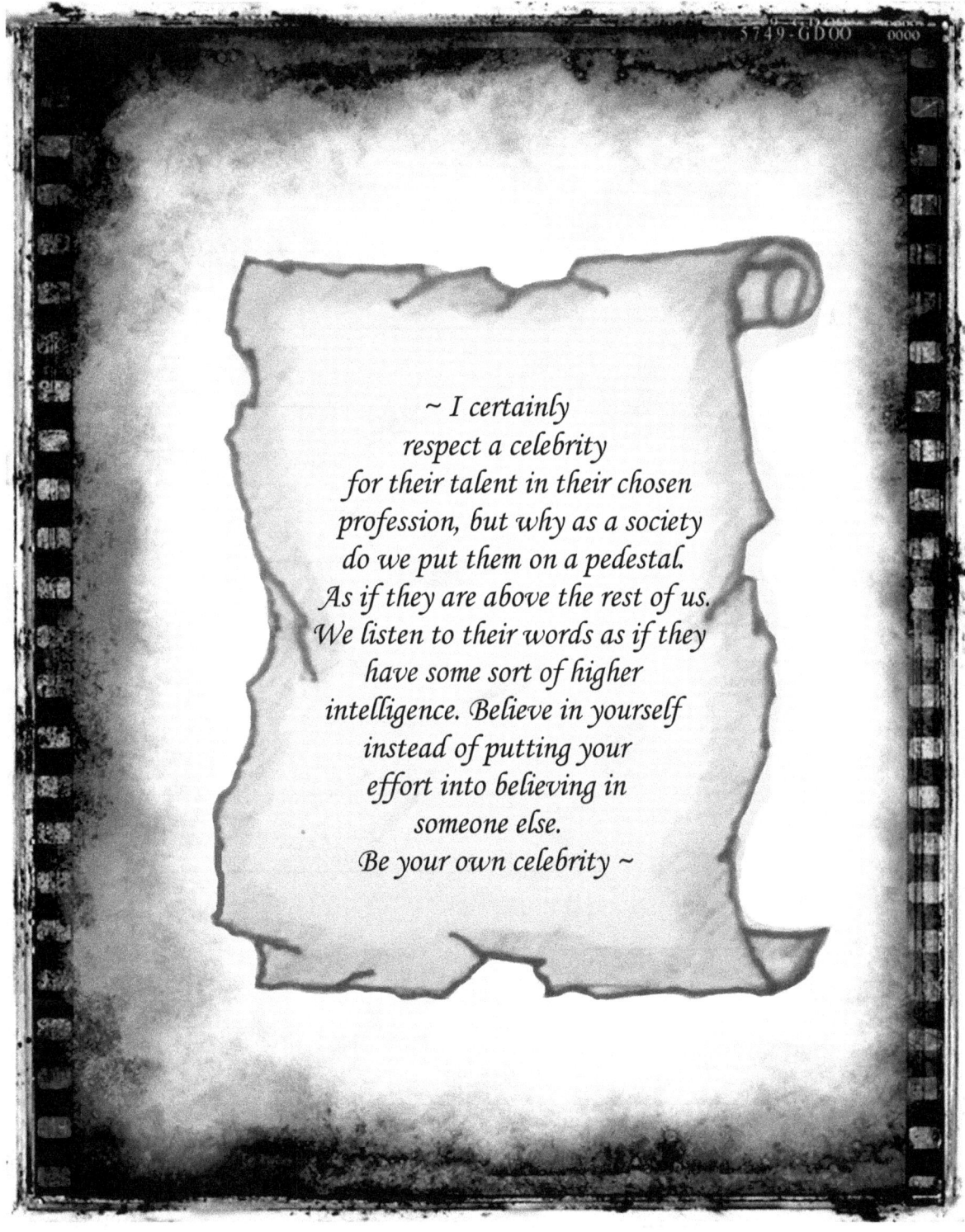

~ I certainly
respect a celebrity
for their talent in their chosen
profession, but why as a society
do we put them on a pedestal.
As if they are above the rest of us.
We listen to their words as if they
have some sort of higher
intelligence. Believe in yourself
instead of putting your
effort into believing in
someone else.
Be your own celebrity ~

Your Thoughts

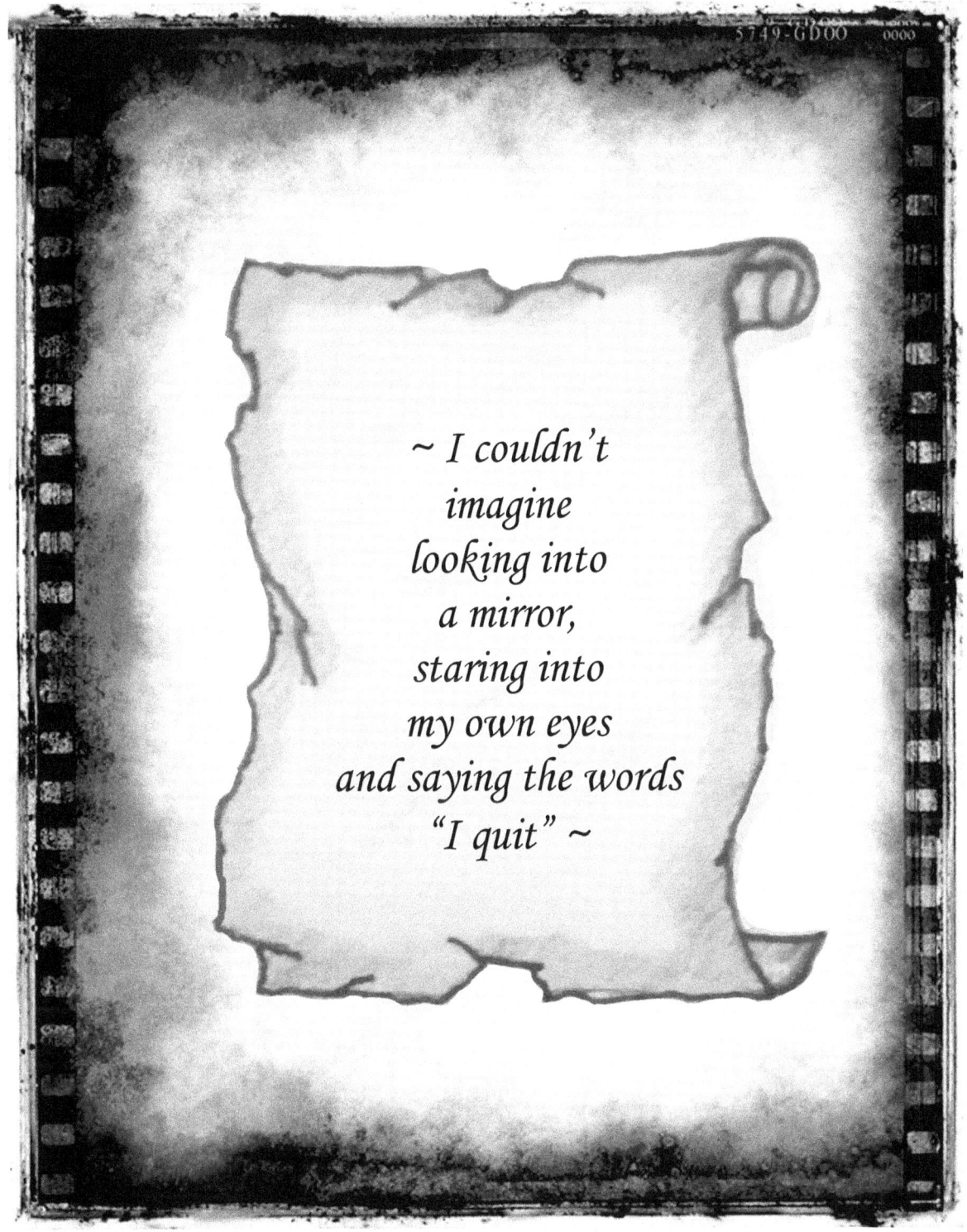

~ I couldn't imagine looking into a mirror, staring into my own eyes and saying the words "I quit" ~

Your Thoughts

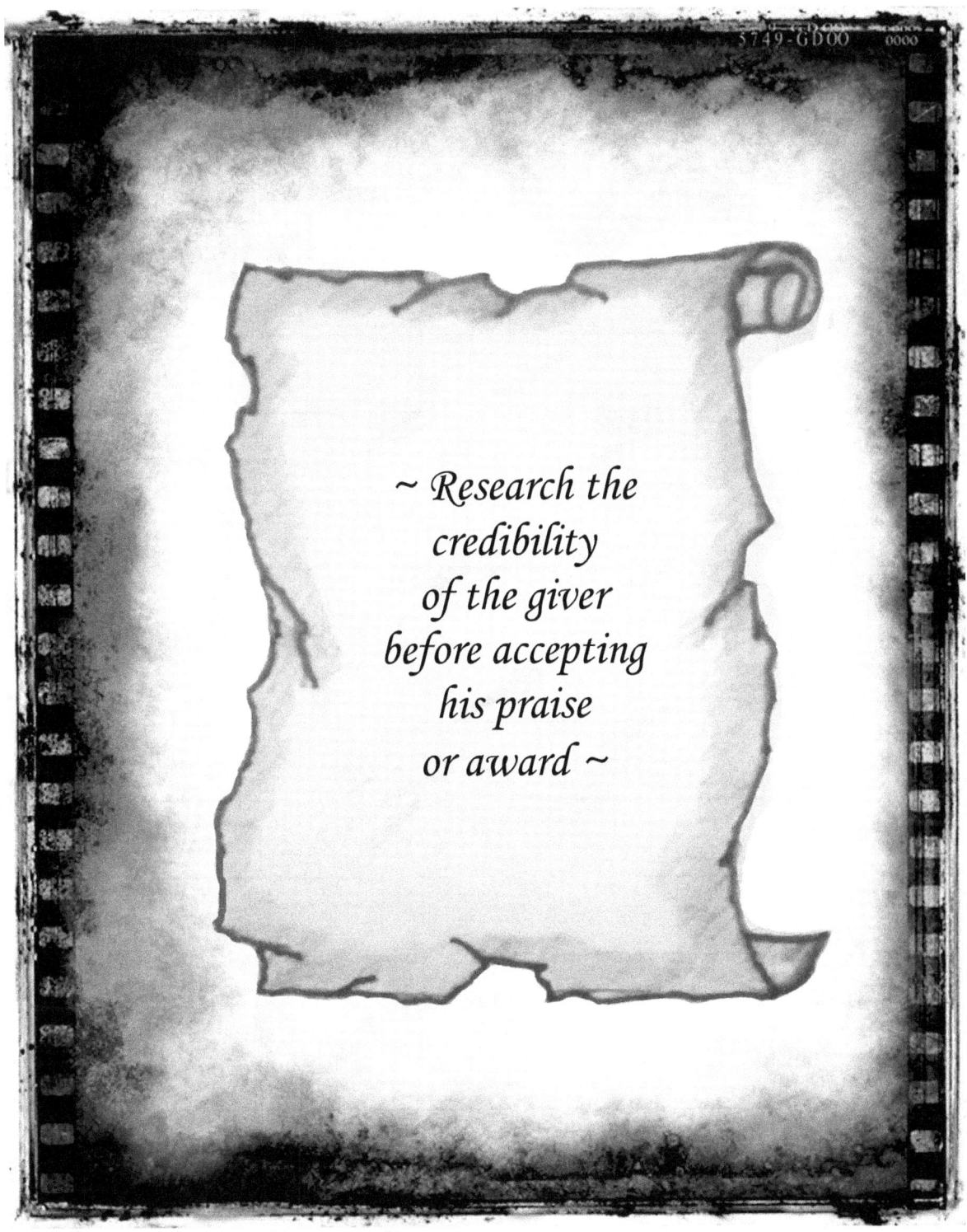

~ Research the credibility of the giver before accepting his praise or award ~

Your Thoughts

~ If you believe people will do everything they say, you will be disappointed more times than not ~

Through The Eyes Of One?

Your Thoughts

~ Go out of your way and try to help or be kind to someone at least once a day, and after a while you will do it without trying ~

Your Thoughts

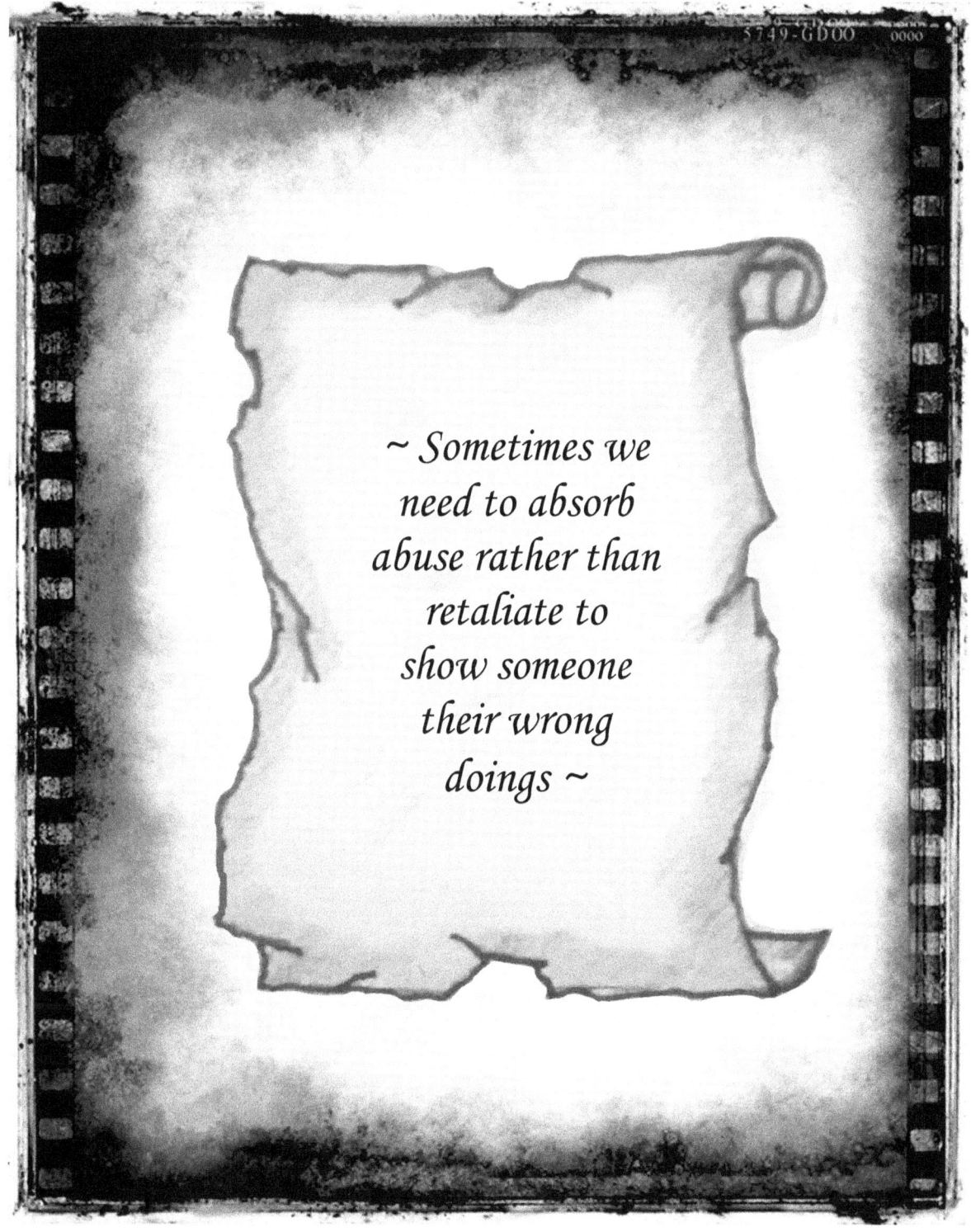

~ Sometimes we need to absorb abuse rather than retaliate to show someone their wrong doings ~

Your Thoughts

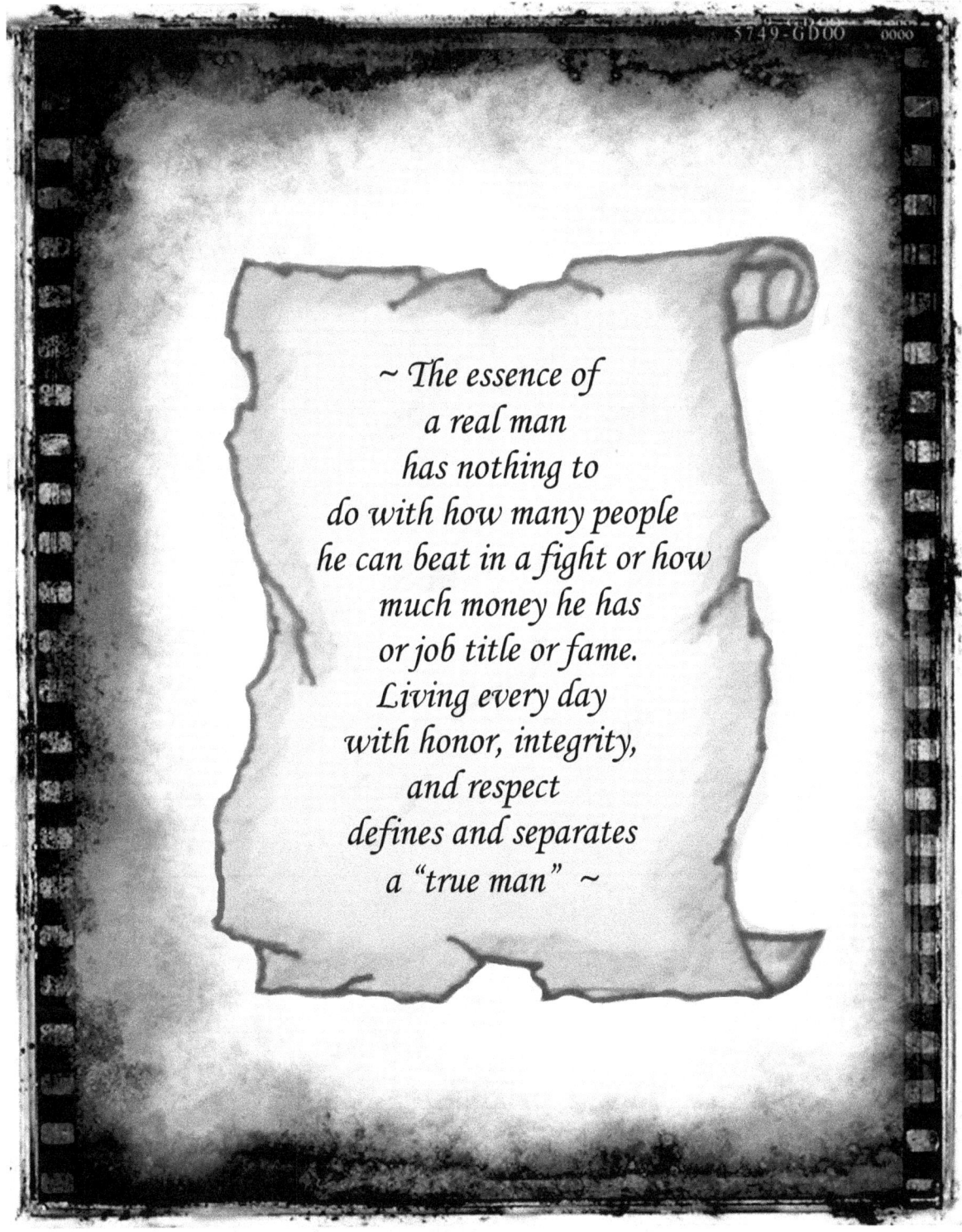

~ The essence of
a real man
has nothing to
do with how many people
he can beat in a fight or how
much money he has
or job title or fame.
Living every day
with honor, integrity,
and respect
defines and separates
a "true man" ~

Your Thoughts

~ Incompetence is too often accepted to the point where it is now expected ~

Your Thoughts

Your Thoughts

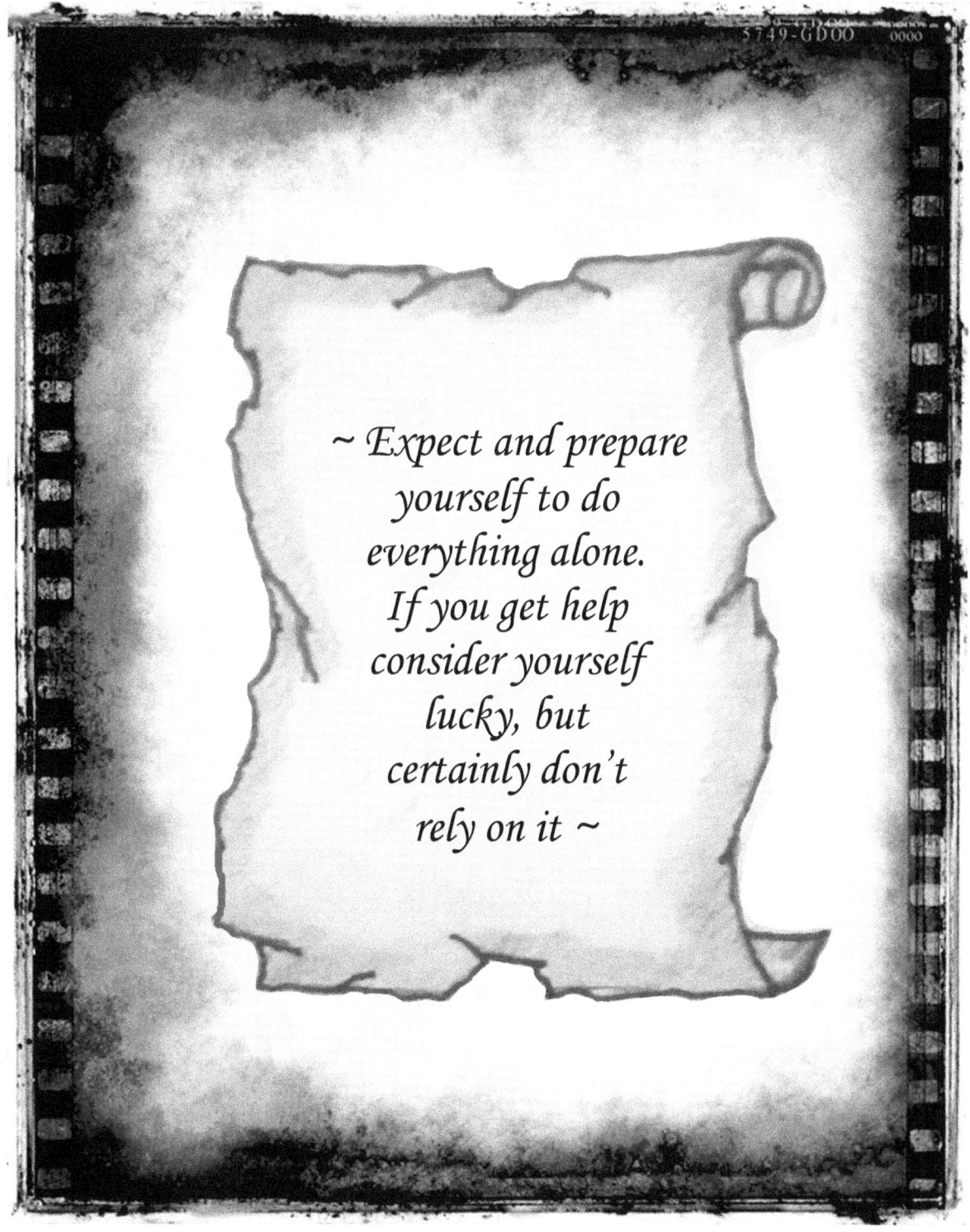

~ Expect and prepare yourself to do everything alone. If you get help consider yourself lucky, but certainly don't rely on it ~

Your Thoughts

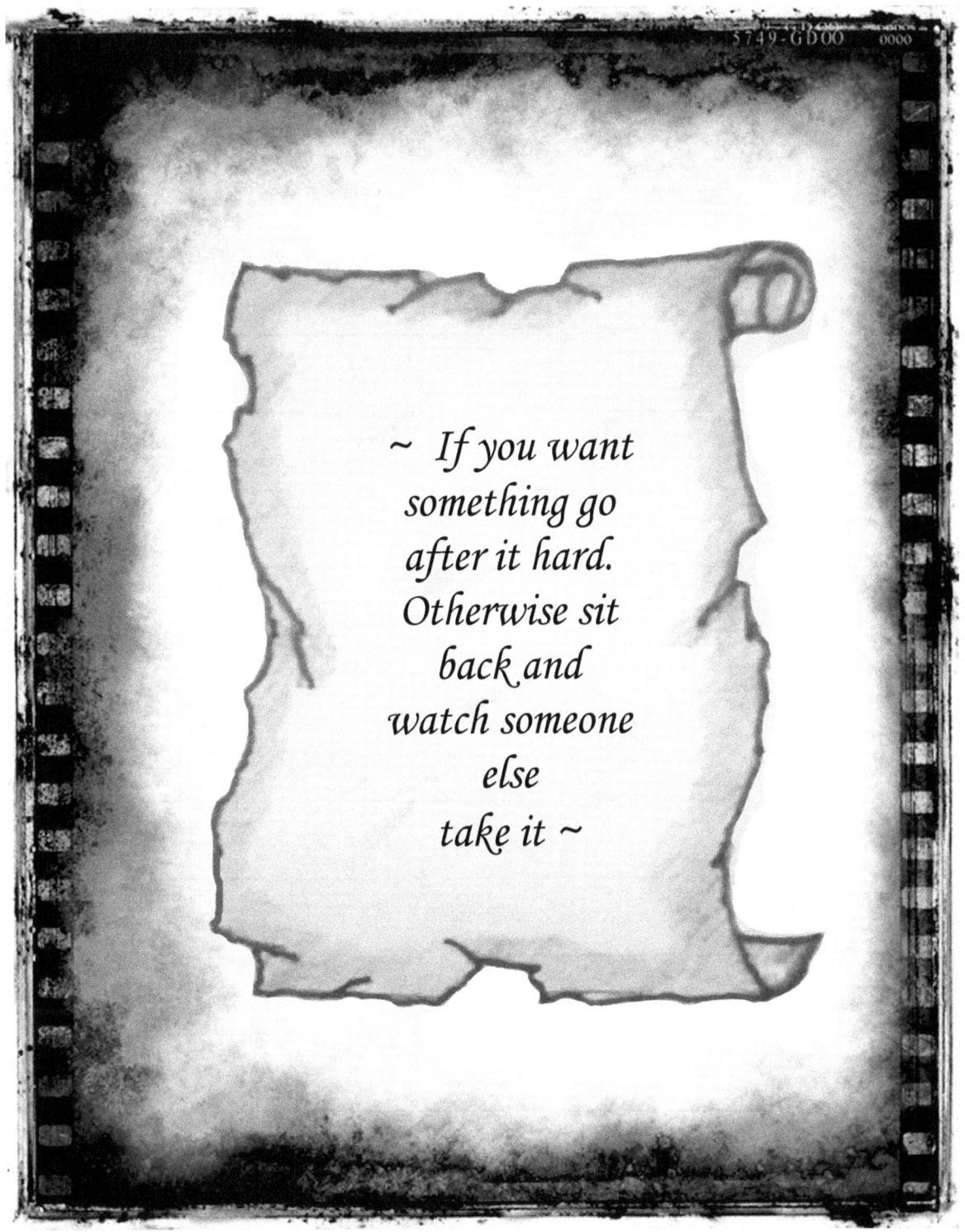

~ If you want something go after it hard. Otherwise sit back and watch someone else take it ~

Your Thoughts

~ Half effort gets you nothing, you might as well not try at all... in the end it's the same result ~

Your Thoughts

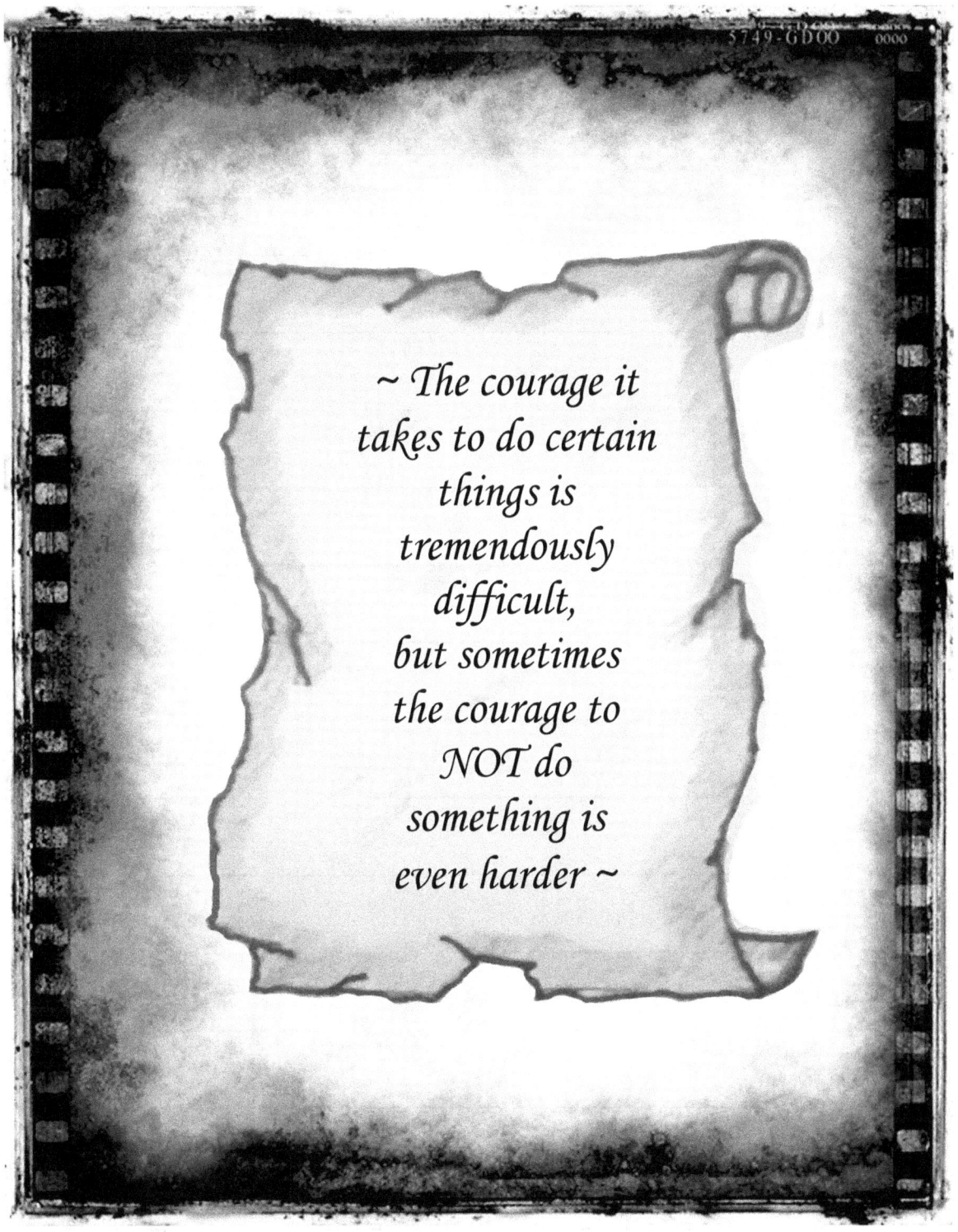

~ The courage it takes to do certain things is tremendously difficult, but sometimes the courage to NOT do something is even harder ~

Your Thoughts

~ You could have everything but if you don't have peace of mind, you have nothing ~

Your Thoughts

~ One needs to prove themselves every day ~

Your Thoughts

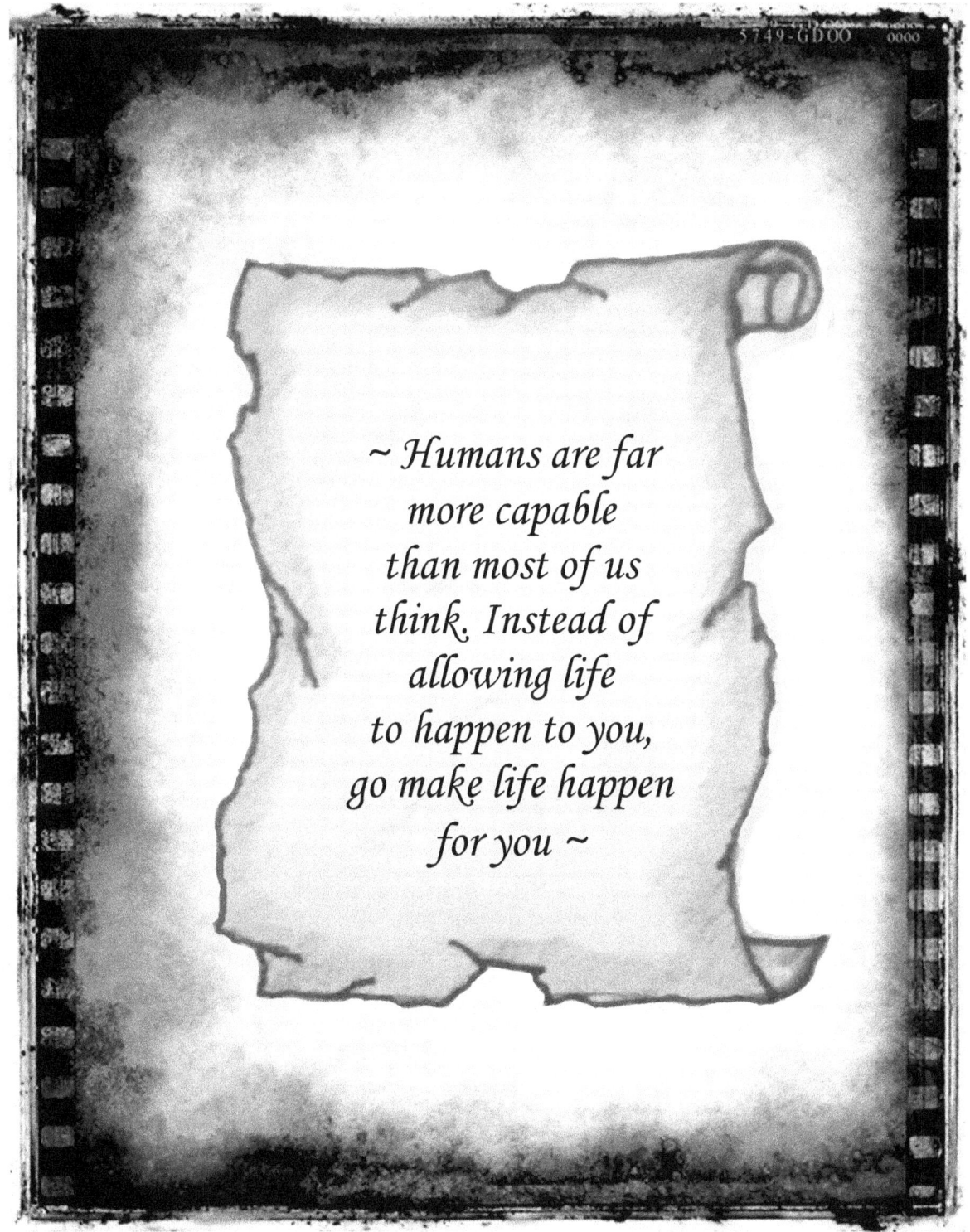

~ Humans are far more capable than most of us think. Instead of allowing life to happen to you, go make life happen for you ~

Your Thoughts

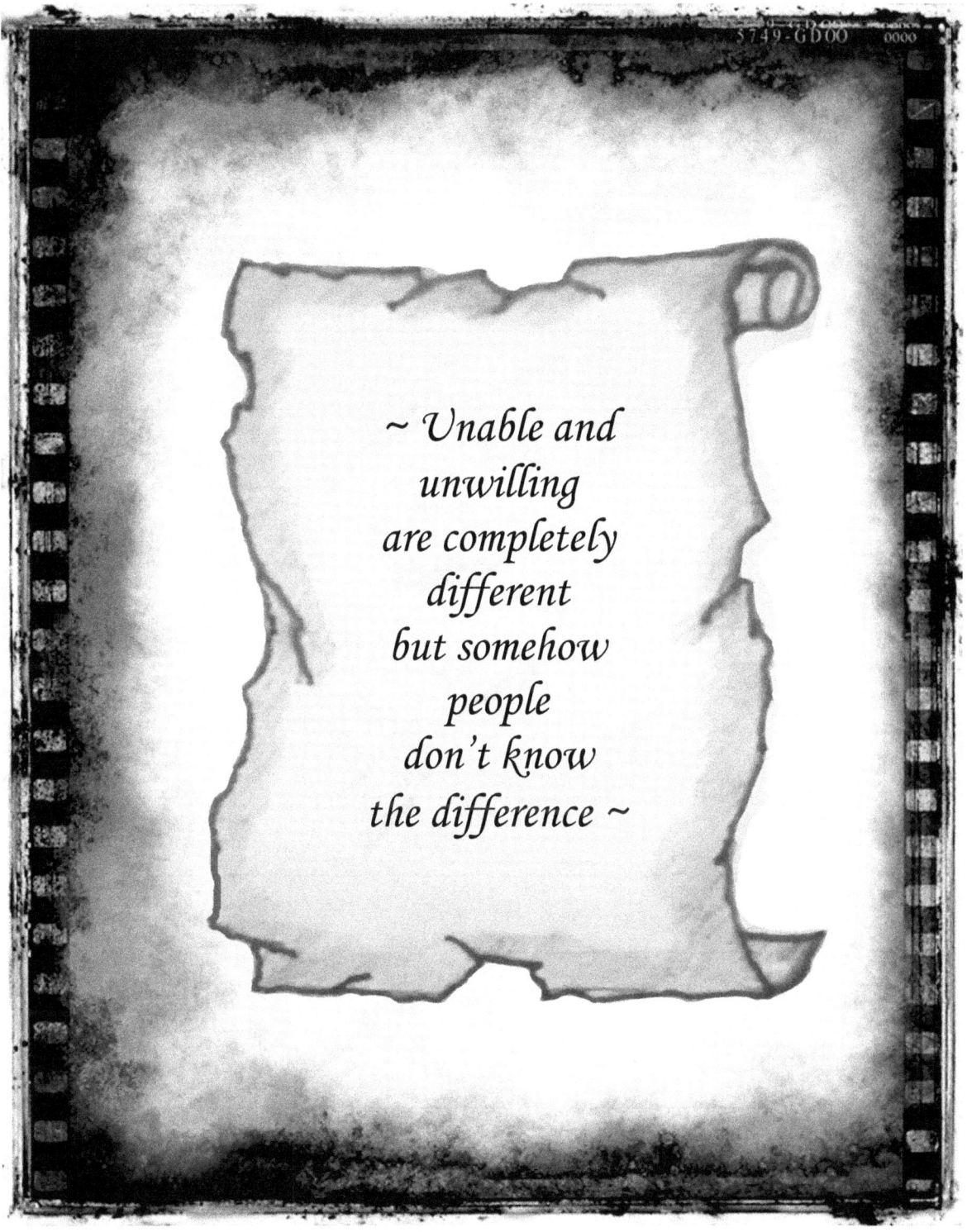
~ Unable and unwilling are completely different but somehow people don't know the difference ~

Your Thoughts

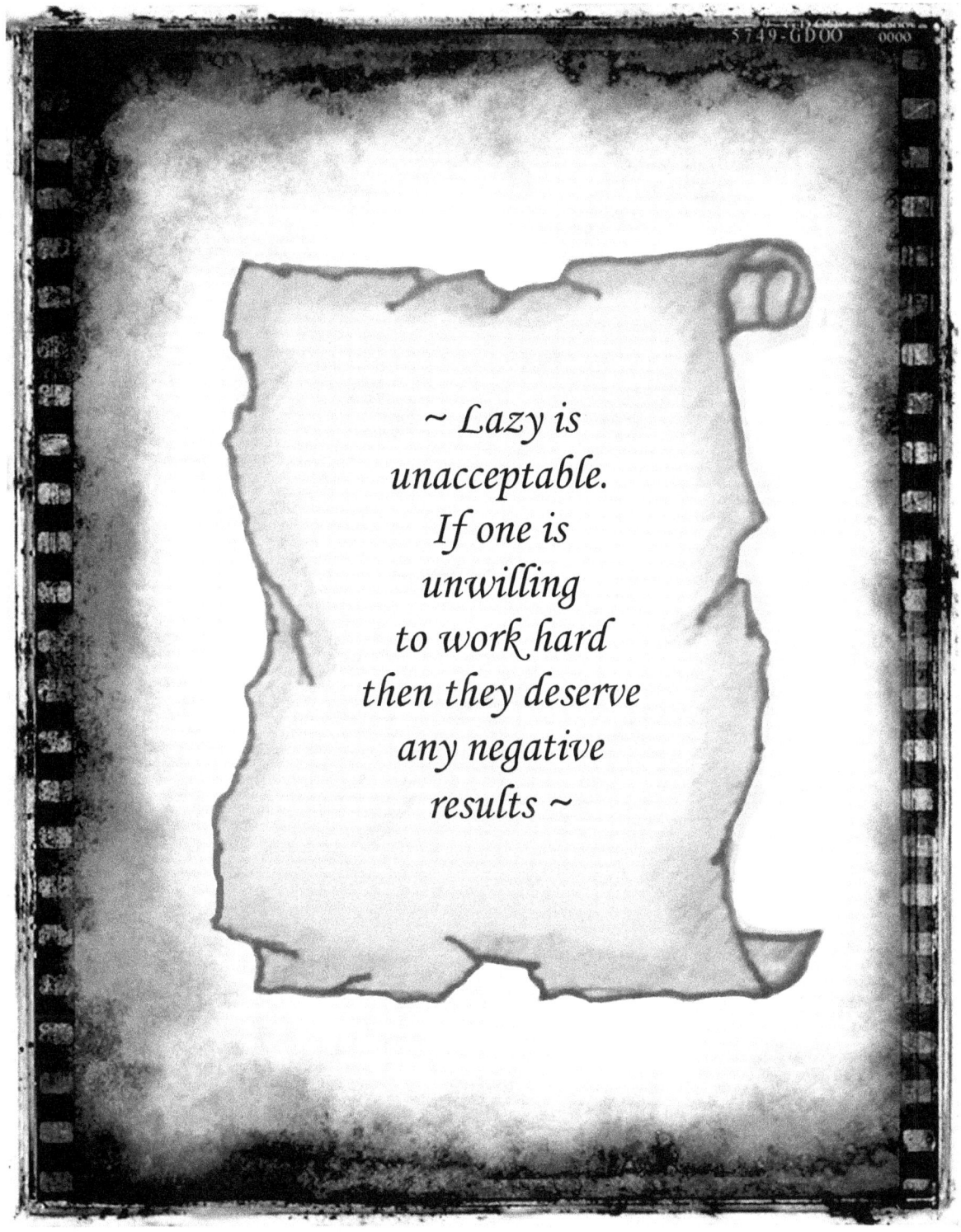

~ Lazy is unacceptable. If one is unwilling to work hard then they deserve any negative results ~

Your Thoughts

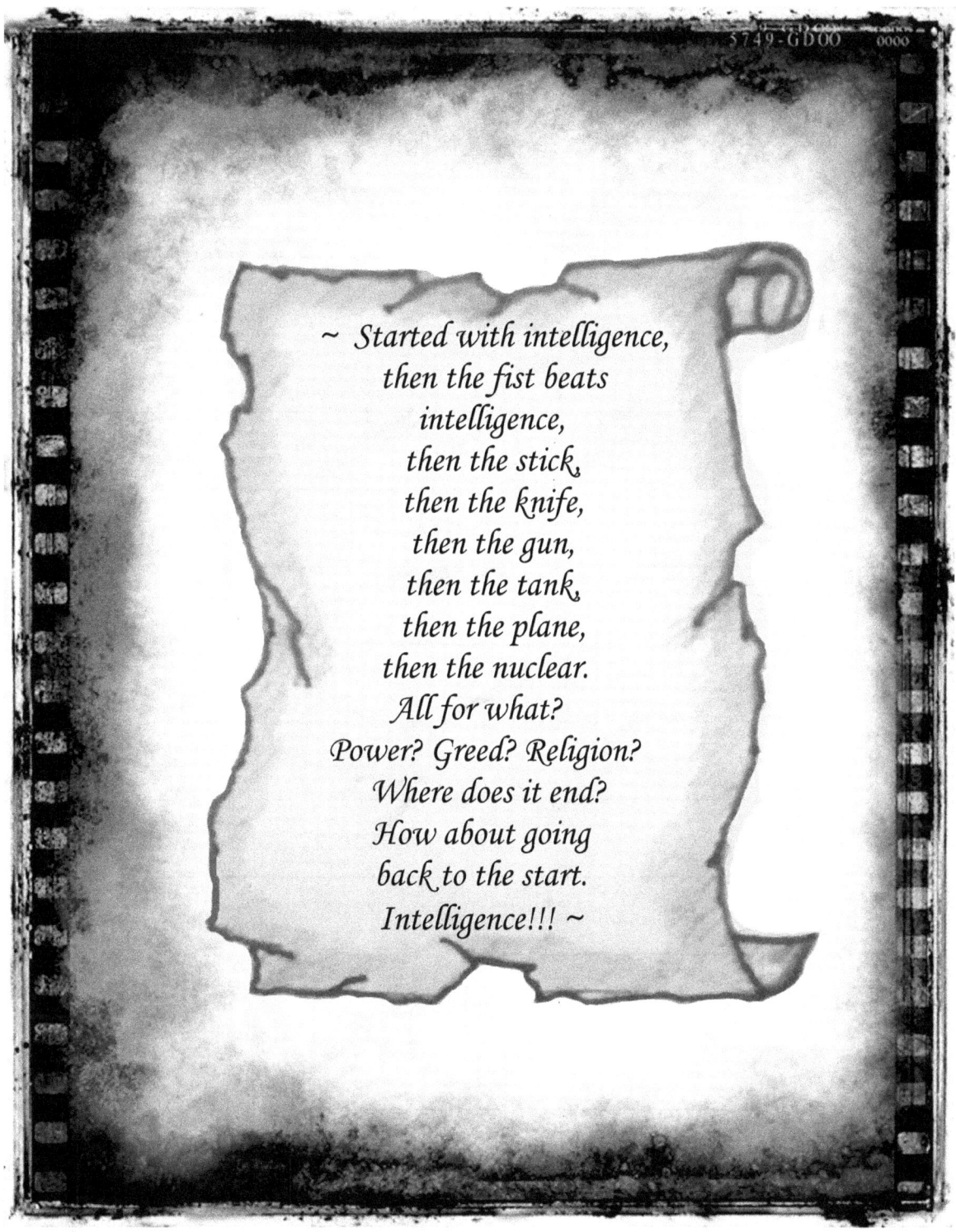

~ Started with intelligence,
then the fist beats
intelligence,
then the stick,
then the knife,
then the gun,
then the tank,
then the plane,
then the nuclear.
All for what?
Power? Greed? Religion?
Where does it end?
How about going
back to the start.
Intelligence!!! ~

Your Thoughts

~ We tell our
children
to use their
words
not their fists
to settle
disagreements,
but what does
every government
on the planet do? ~

Your Thoughts

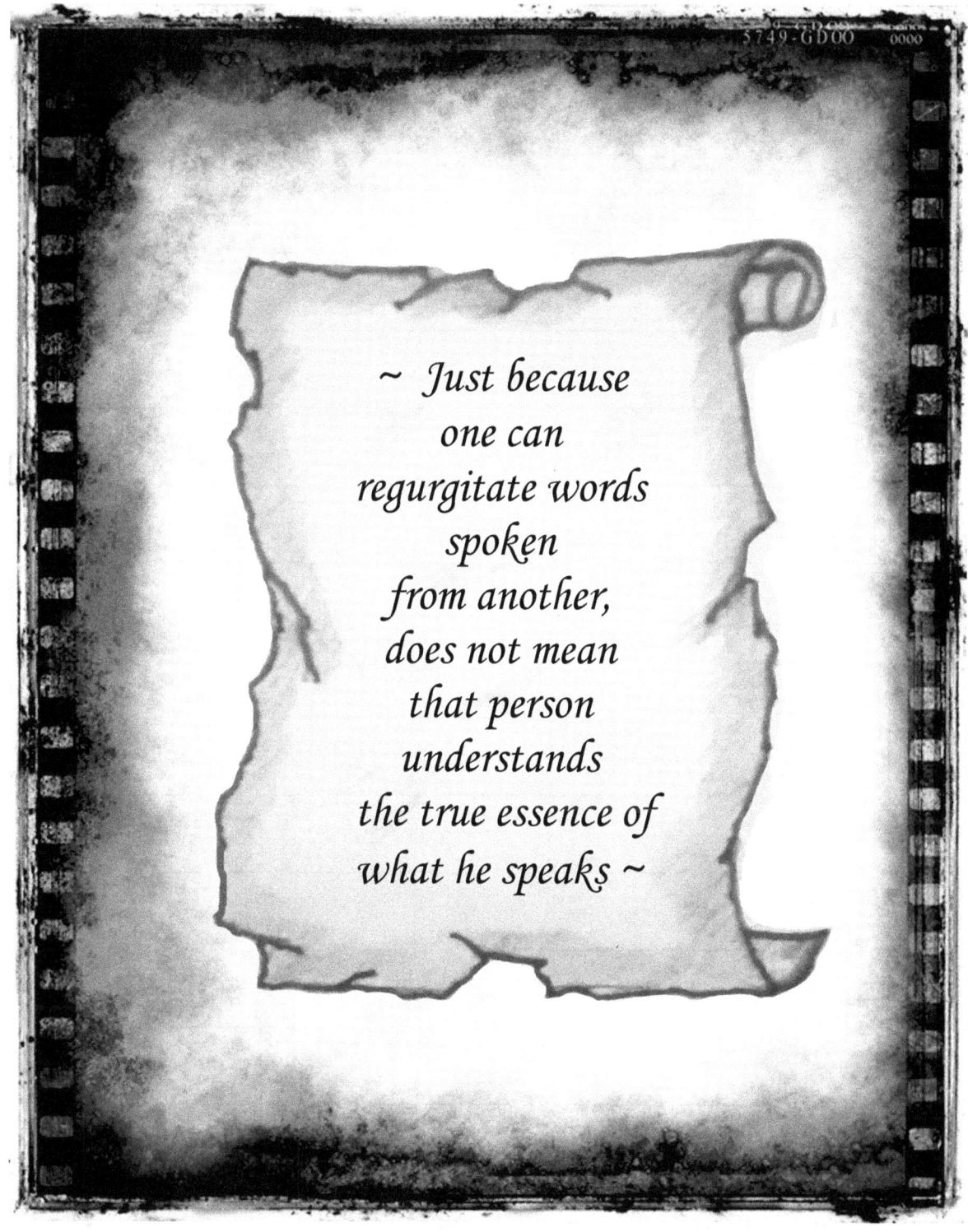

~ Just because one can regurgitate words spoken from another, does not mean that person understands the true essence of what he speaks ~

Your Thoughts

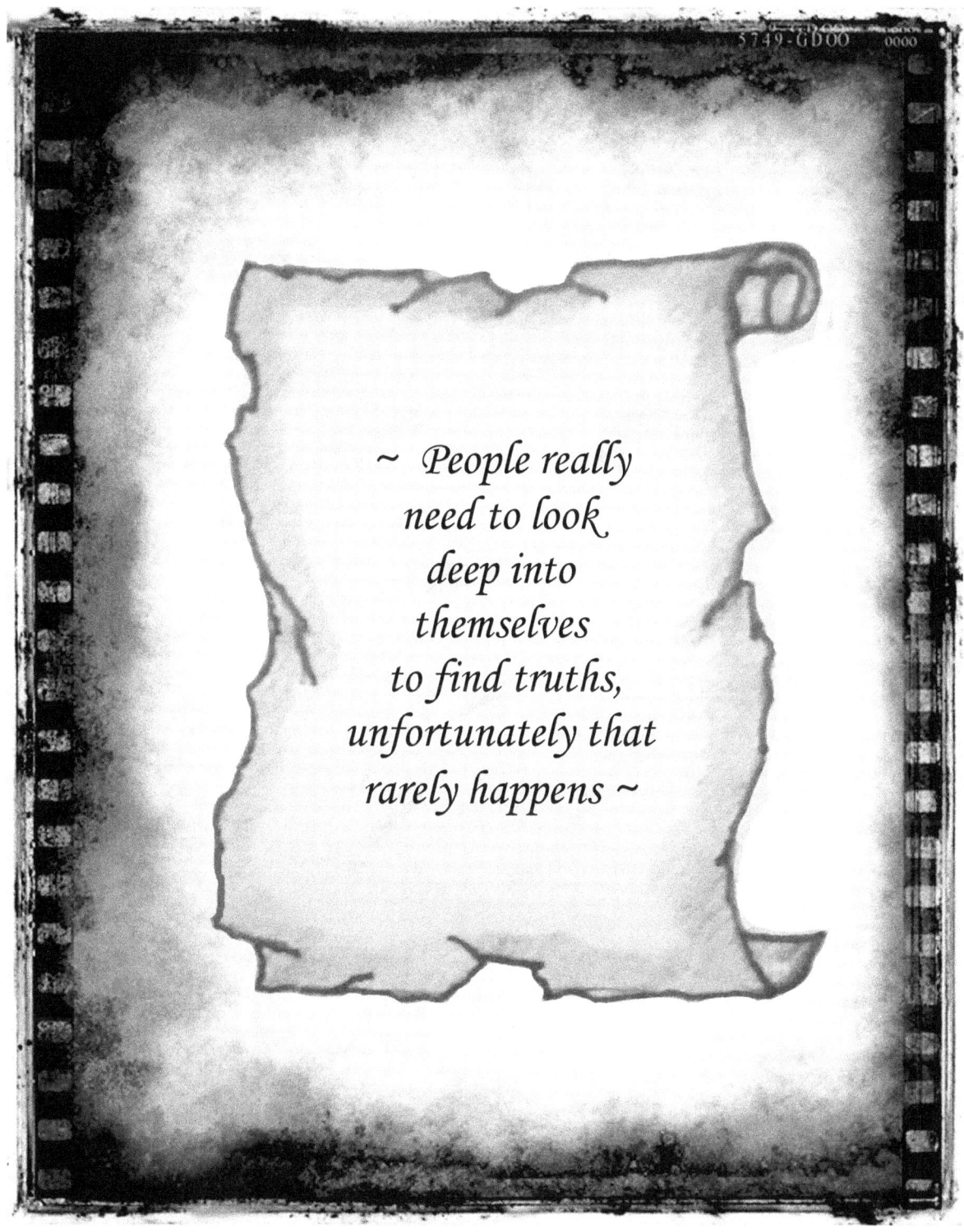

*~ People really
need to look
deep into
themselves
to find truths,
unfortunately that
rarely happens ~*

Your Thoughts

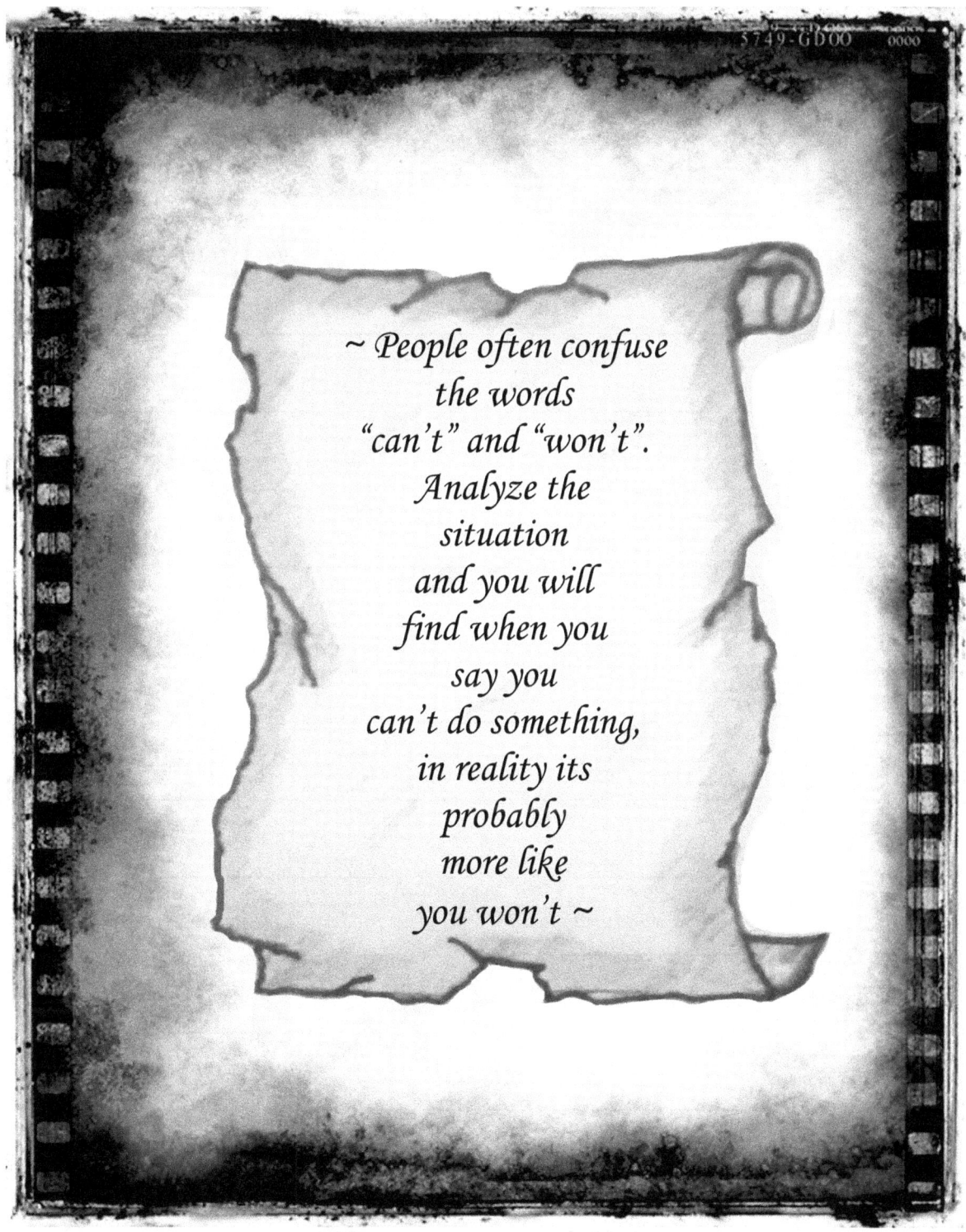

~ People often confuse the words "can't" and "won't". Analyze the situation and you will find when you say you can't do something, in reality its probably more like you won't ~

Your Thoughts

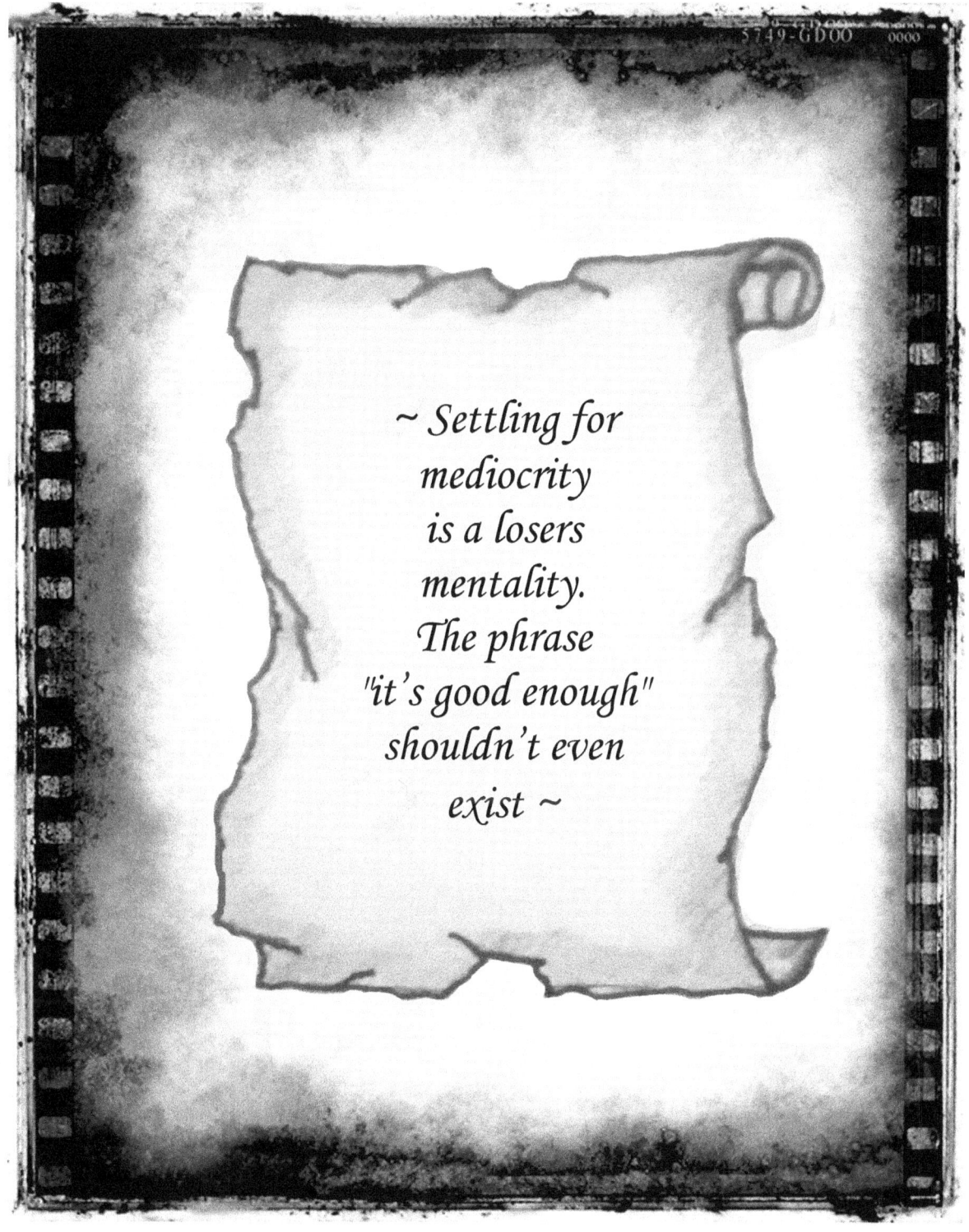

~ Settling for mediocrity is a losers mentality. The phrase "it's good enough" shouldn't even exist ~

Your Thoughts

~ Don't deflect your short comings onto someone else. Own up to your own actions or words ~

Your Thoughts

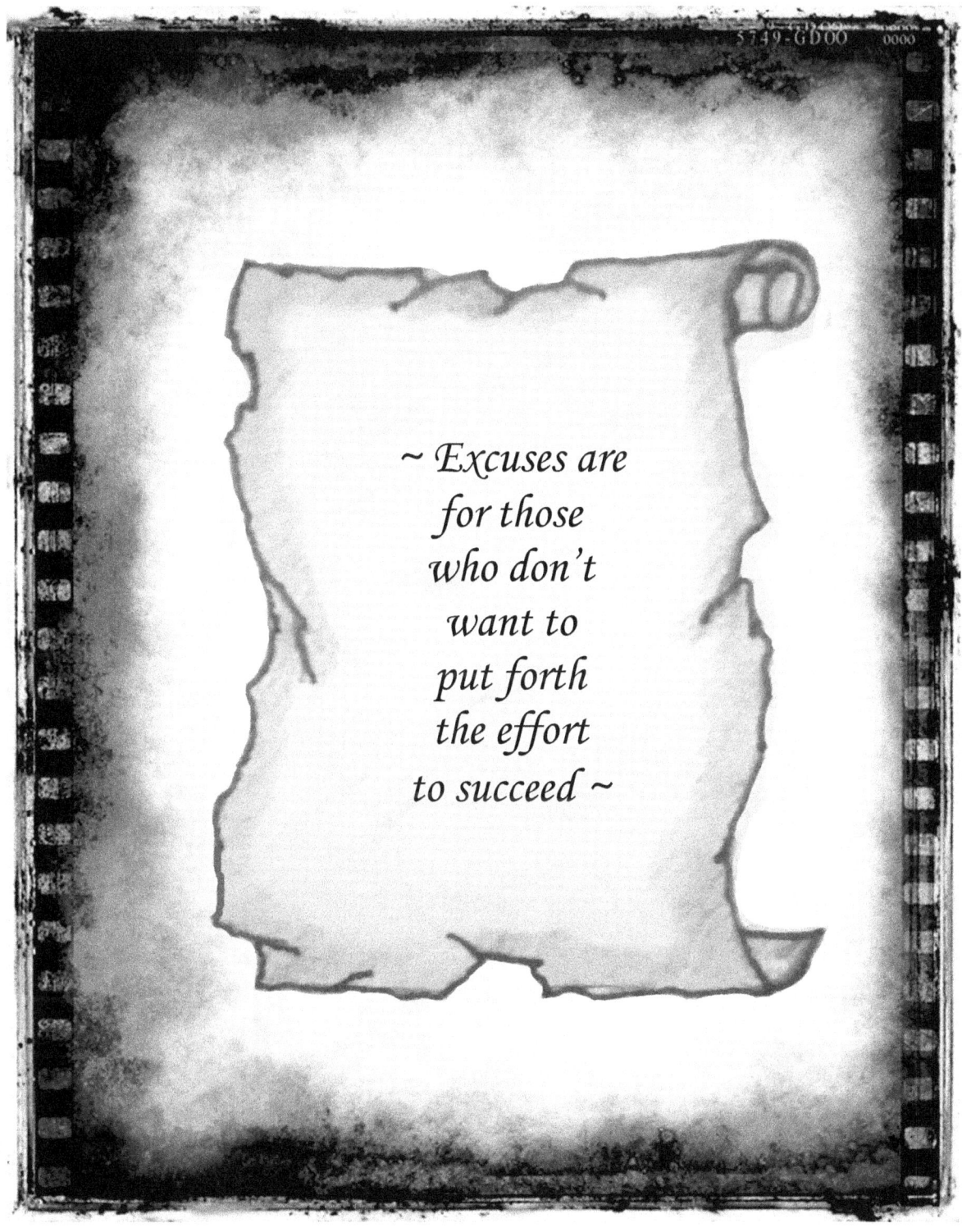

~ Excuses are for those who don't want to put forth the effort to succeed ~

Through The Eyes Of One?

<u>Your Thoughts</u>

Your Thoughts

~ There is always someone who wants to see you fail. For whatever reason, maybe it's jealousy, maybe it's their own insecurities. Either way, let their lack of desire fuel yours ~

Your Thoughts

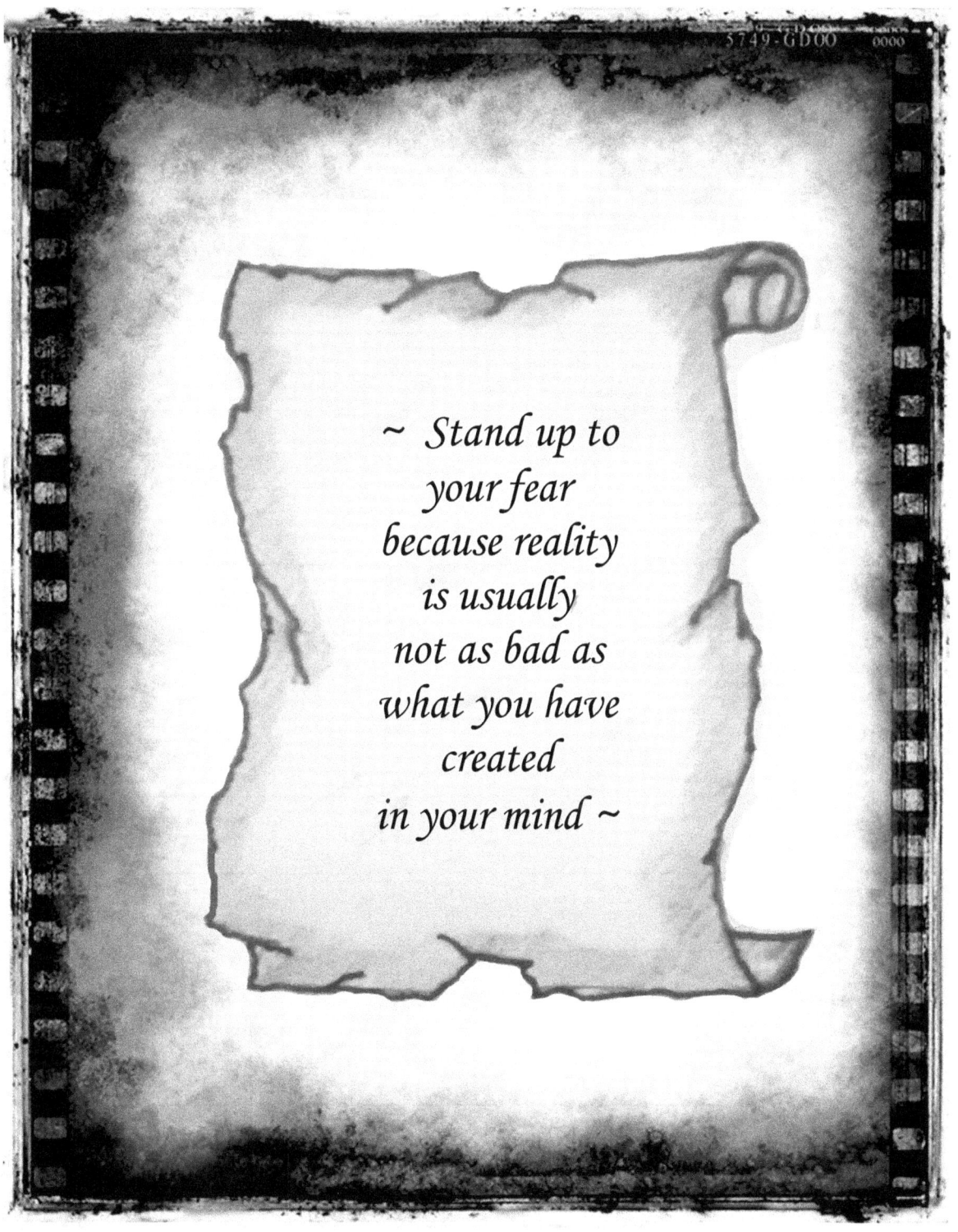

~ Stand up to
your fear
because reality
is usually
not as bad as
what you have
created
in your mind ~

Your Thoughts

~ If evil had roots, selfishness would be the seed ~

Your Thoughts

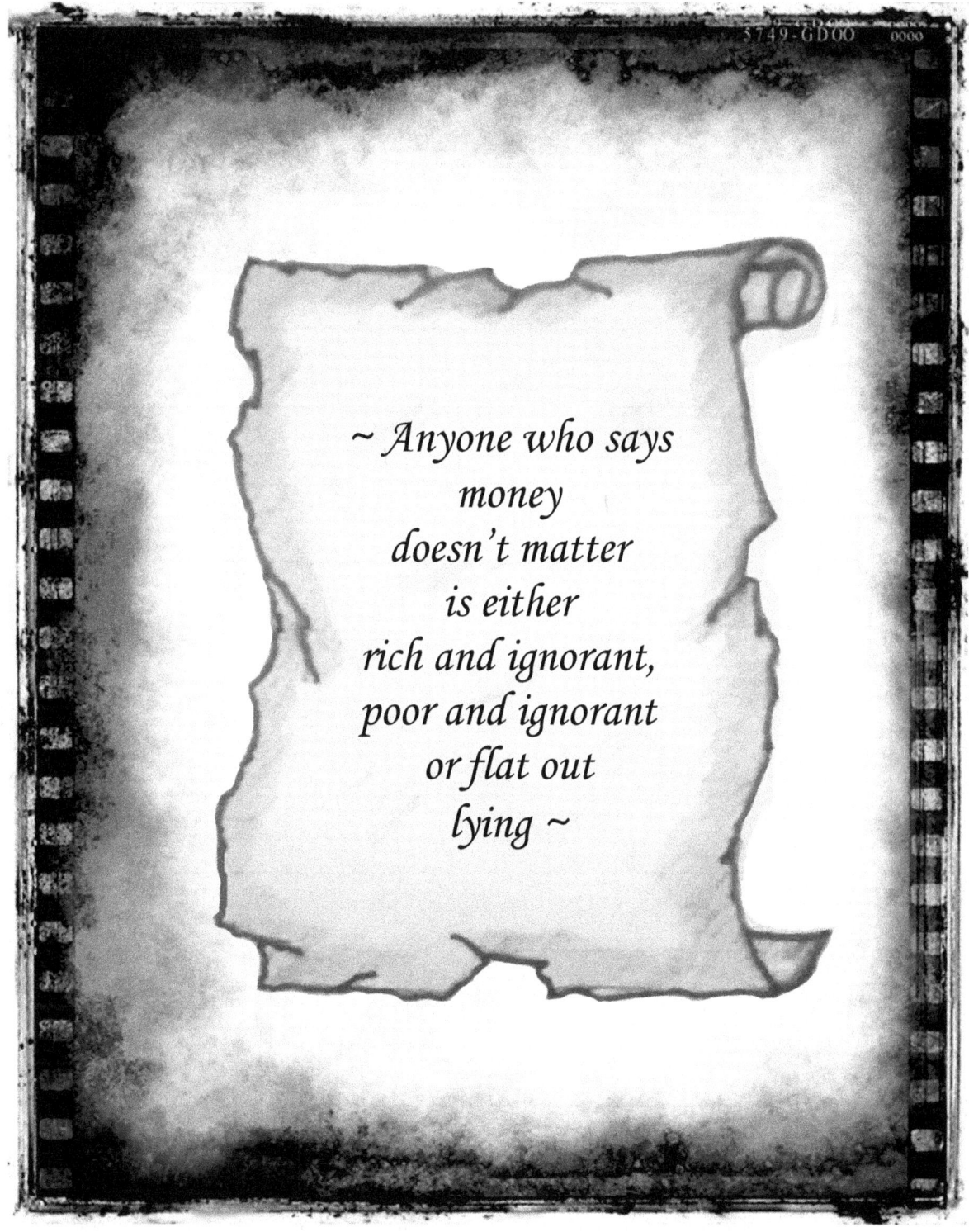

~ Anyone who says
money
doesn't matter
is either
rich and ignorant,
poor and ignorant
or flat out
lying ~

Your Thoughts

~ Peace of mind is the root of happiness ~

Your Thoughts

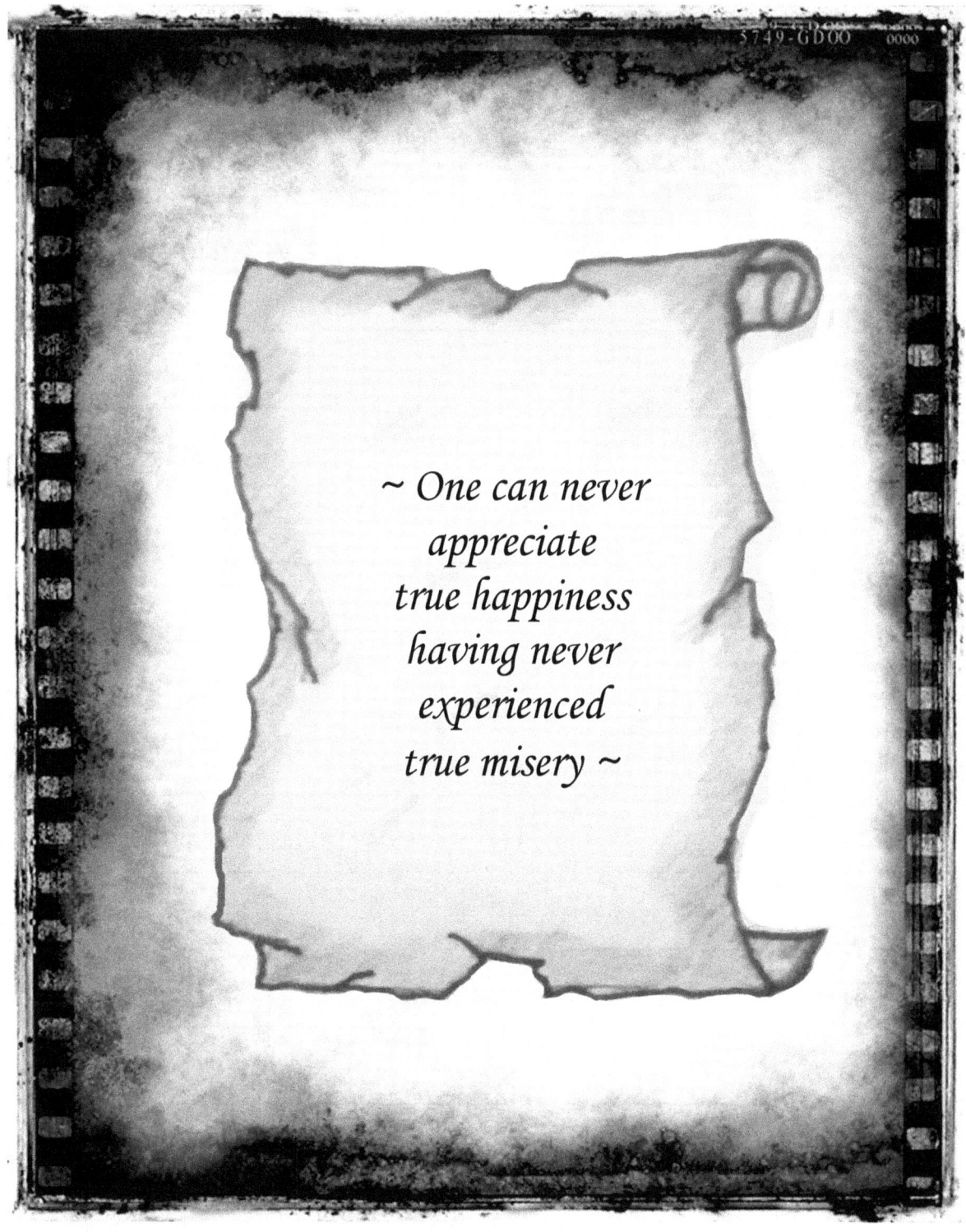

~ One can never appreciate true happiness having never experienced true misery ~

Your Thoughts

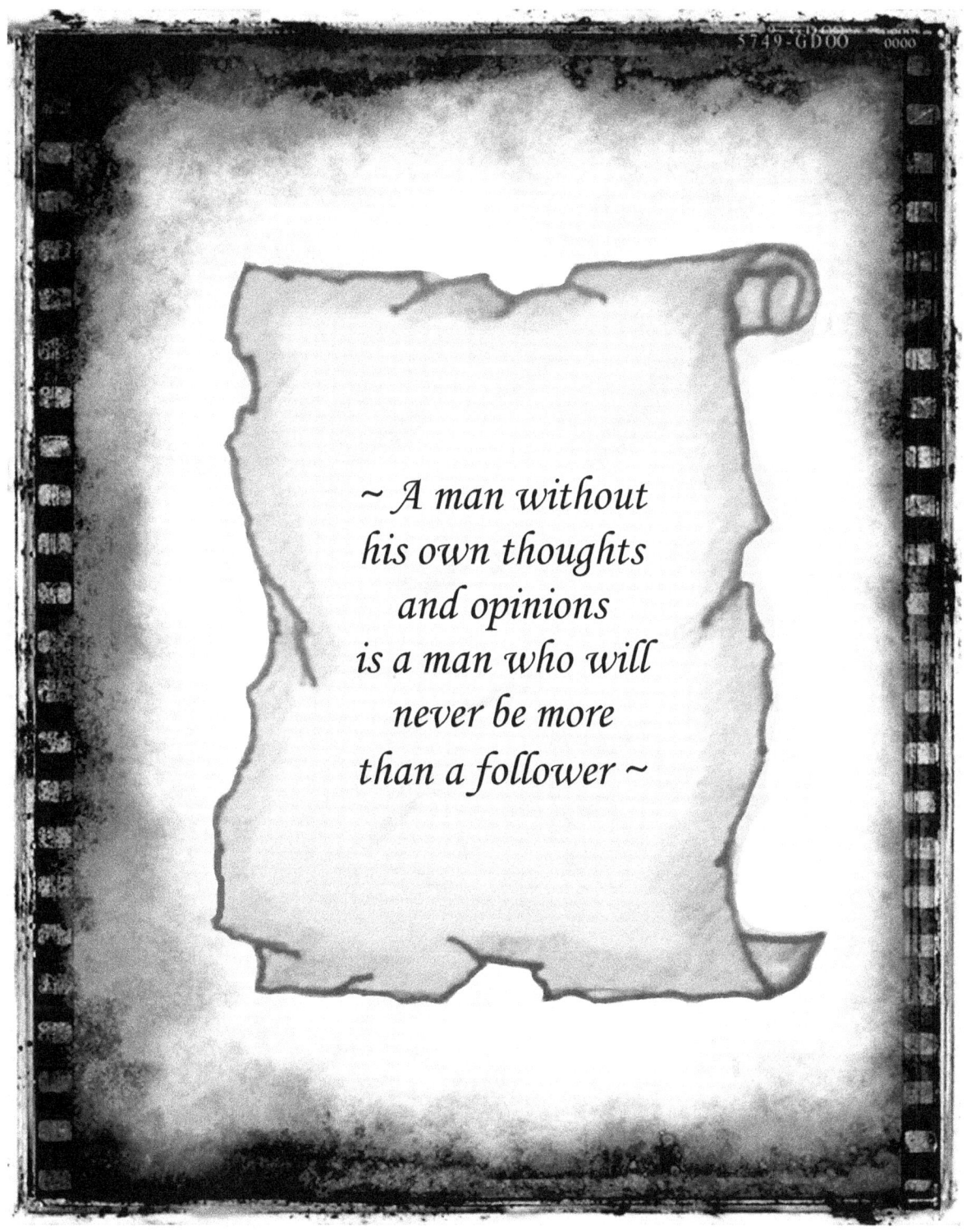

~ *A man without his own thoughts and opinions is a man who will never be more than a follower* ~

Your Thoughts

~ Failure does
not make you
a loser.
Quitting does ~

Your Thoughts

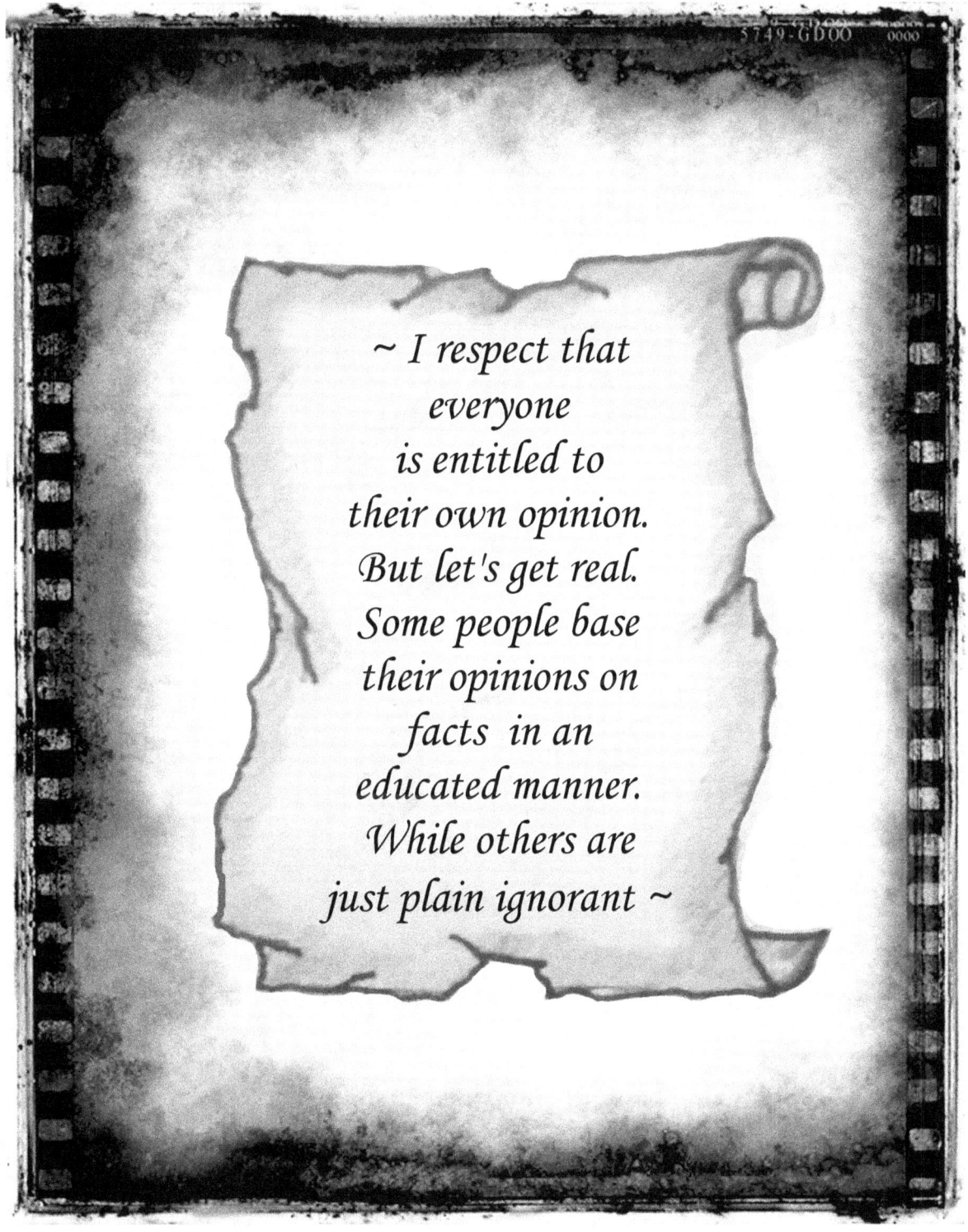

~ I respect that everyone is entitled to their own opinion. But let's get real. Some people base their opinions on facts in an educated manner. While others are just plain ignorant ~

Your Thoughts

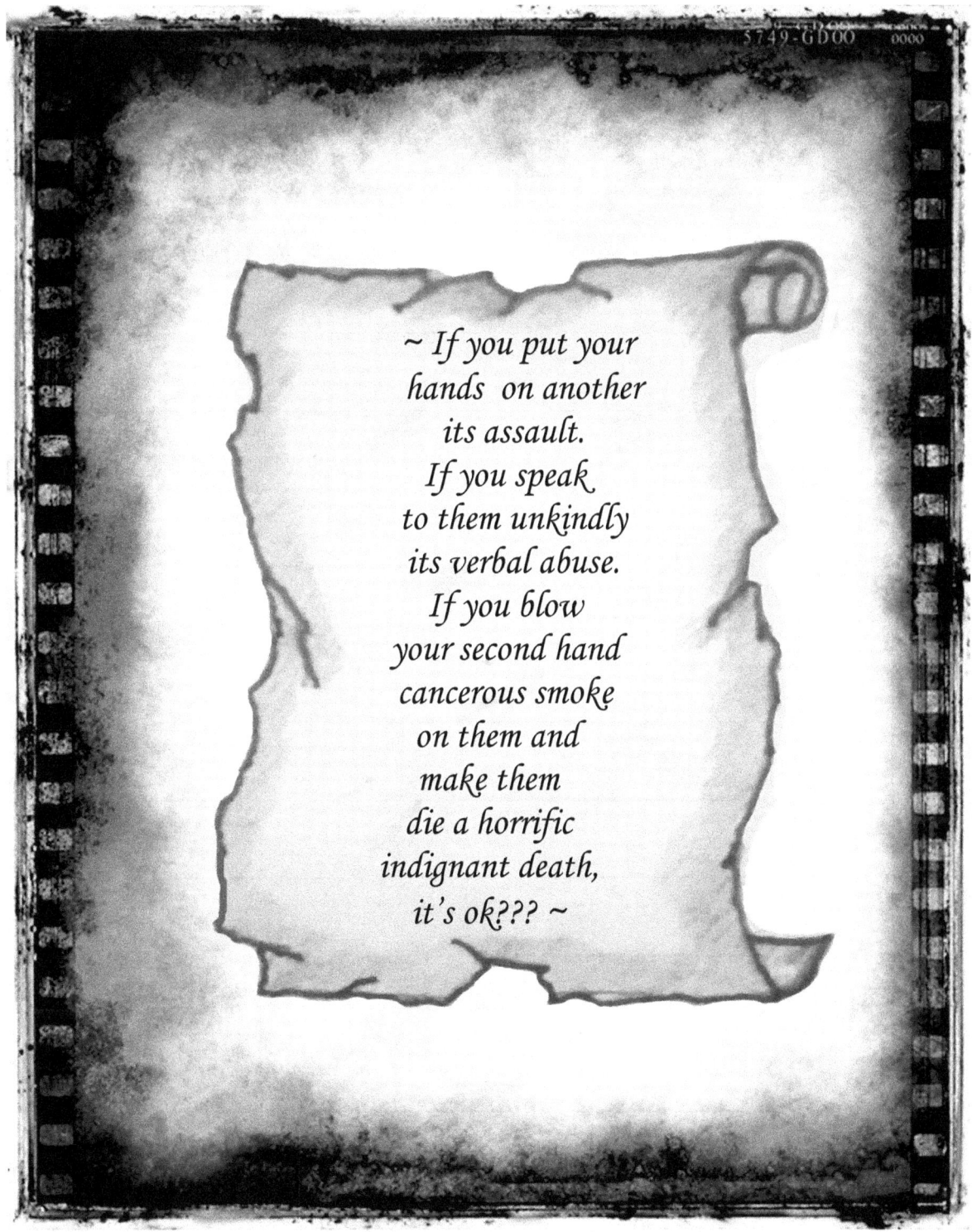

~ If you put your
hands on another
its assault.
If you speak
to them unkindly
its verbal abuse.
If you blow
your second hand
cancerous smoke
on them and
make them
die a horrific
indignant death,
it's ok??? ~

Your Thoughts

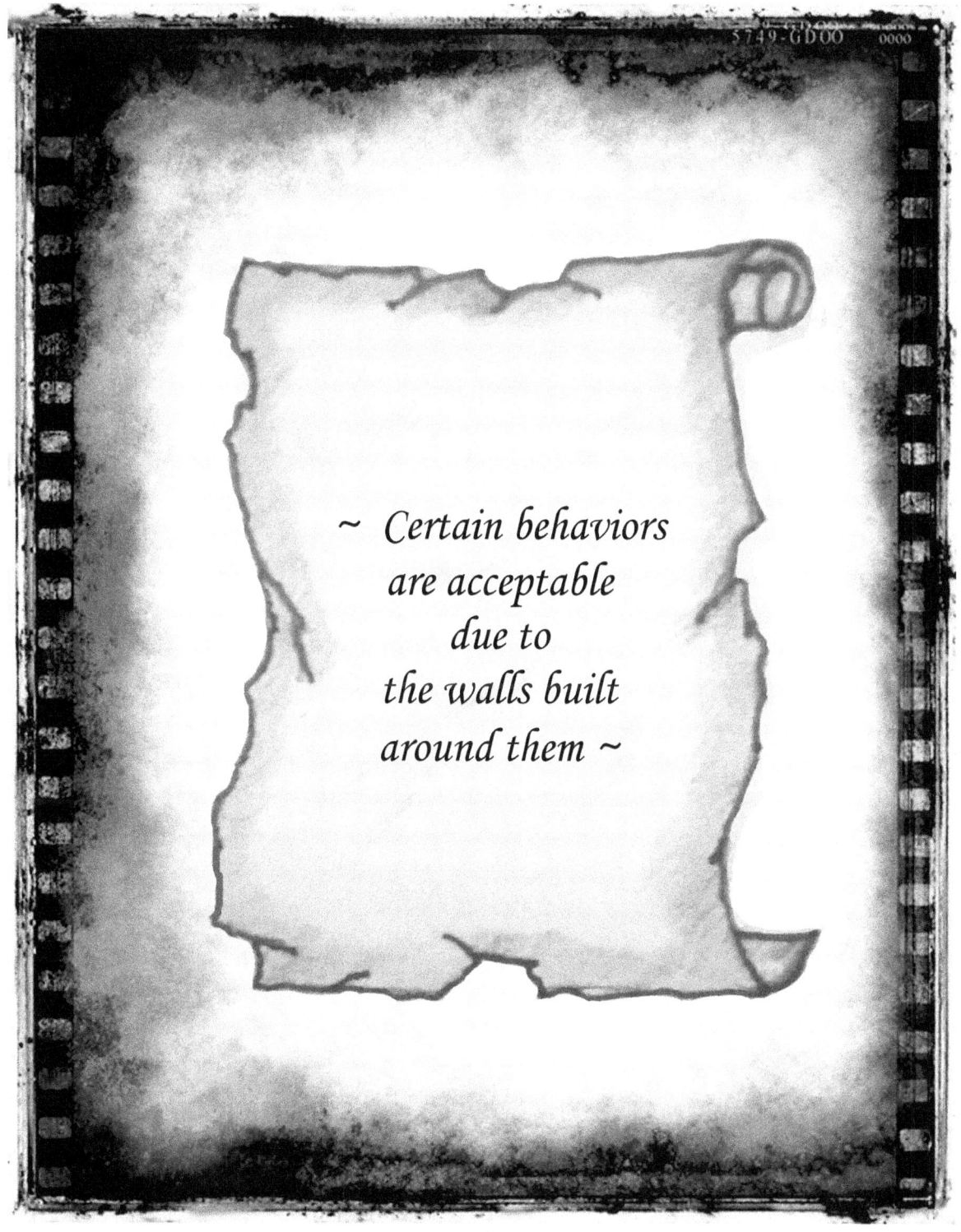

~ Certain behaviors
are acceptable
due to
the walls built
around them ~

Your Thoughts

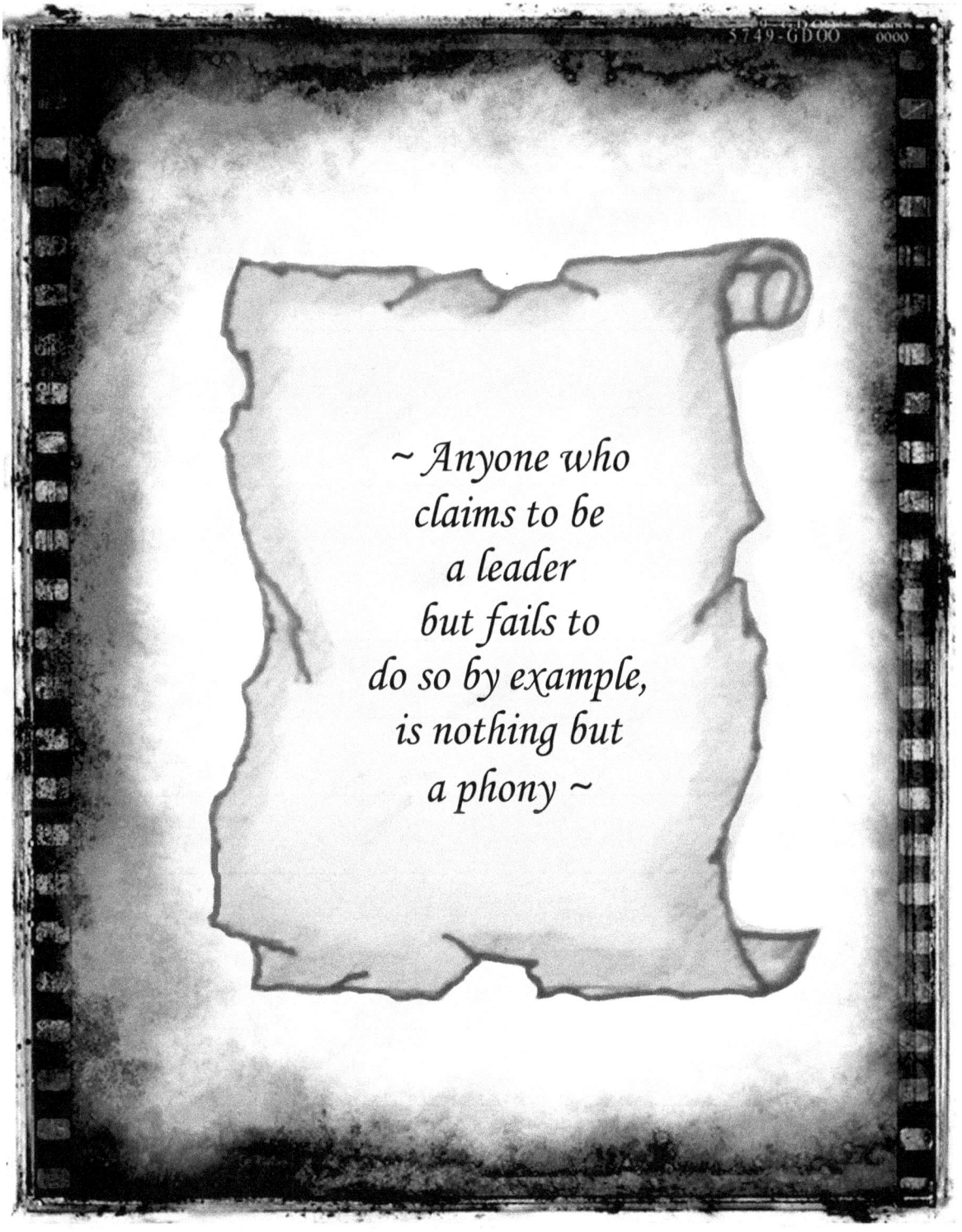

~ Anyone who
claims to be
a leader
but fails to
do so by example,
is nothing but
a phony ~

Your Thoughts

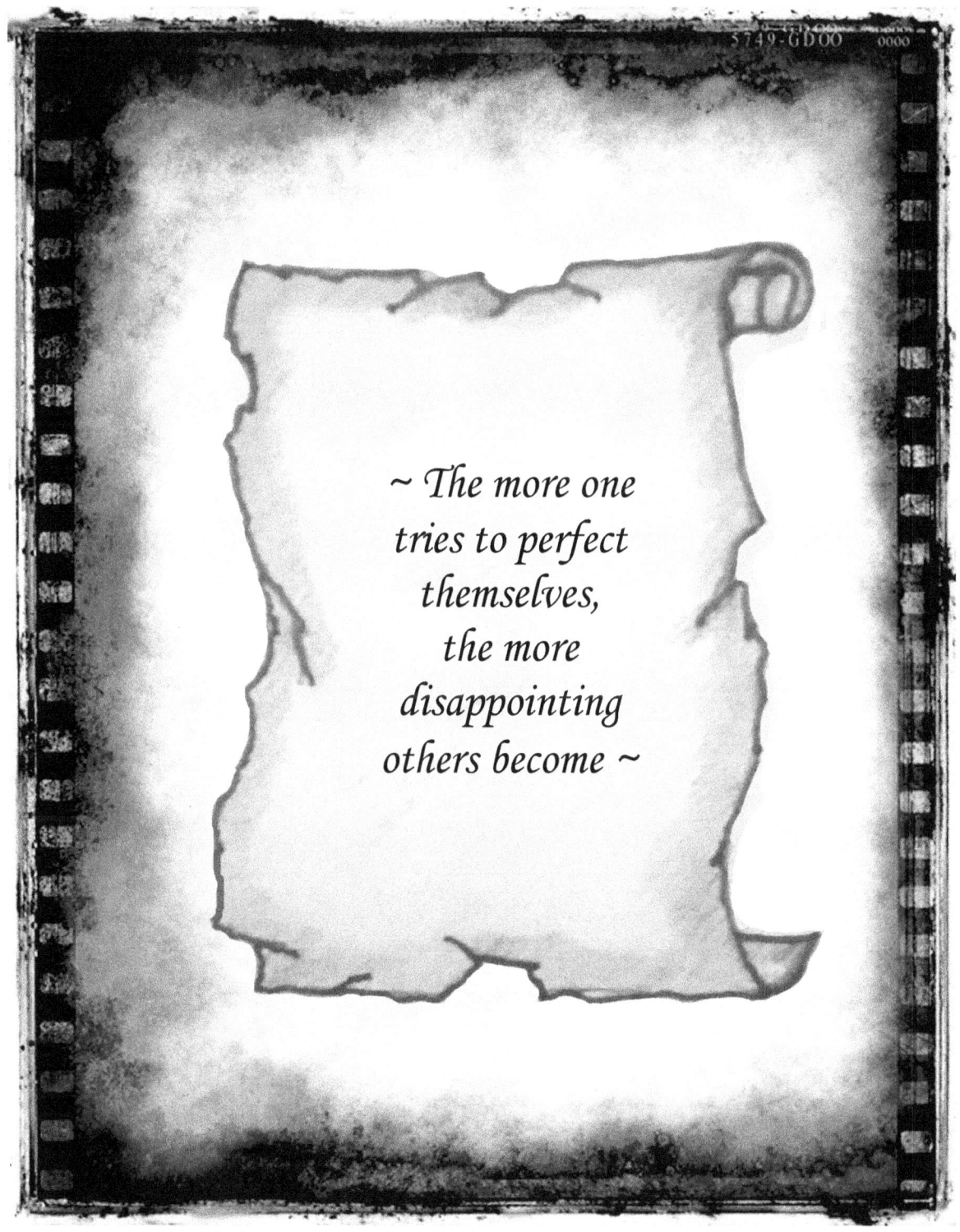

~ The more one tries to perfect themselves, the more disappointing others become ~

Your Thoughts

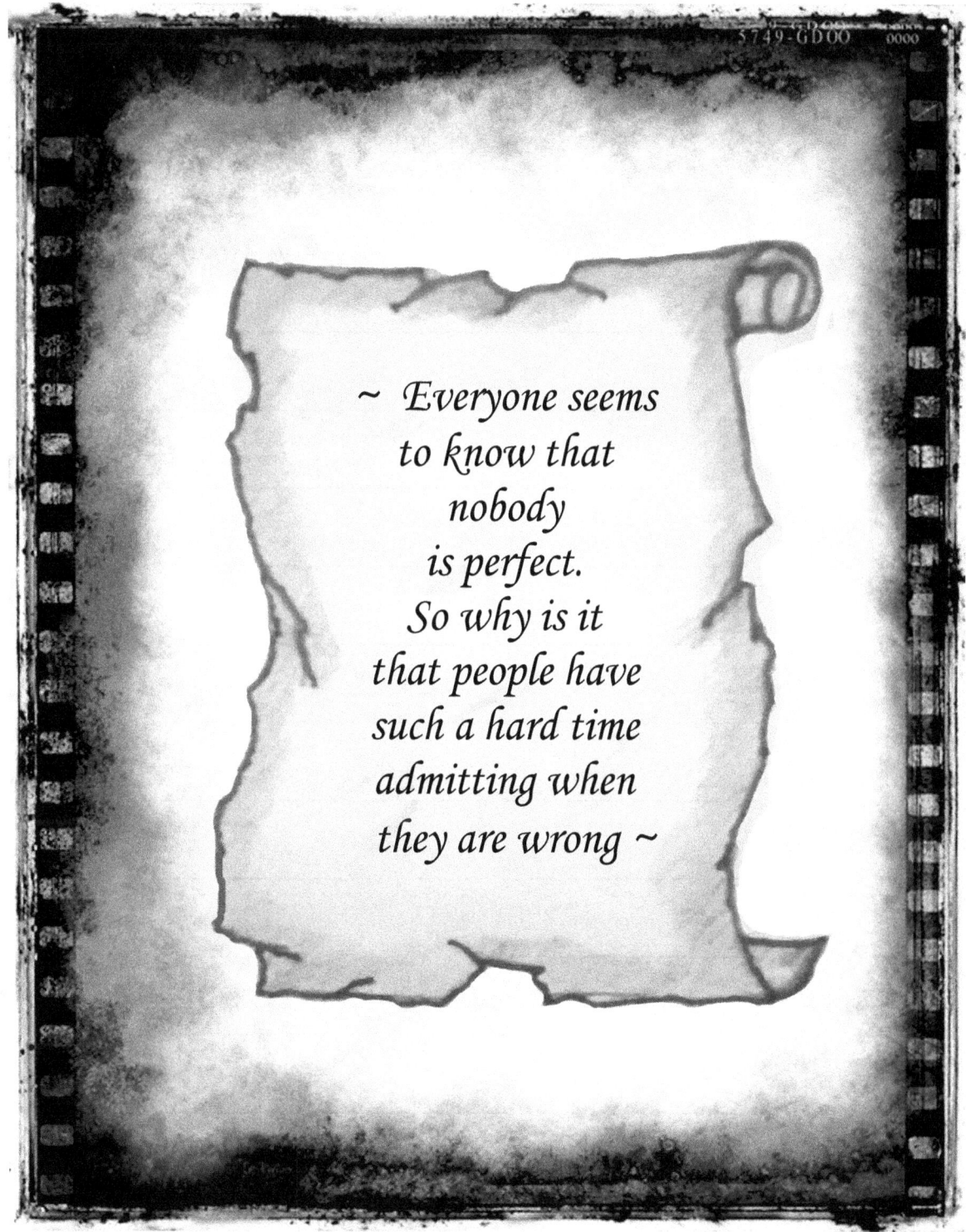

~ Everyone seems
to know that
nobody
is perfect.
So why is it
that people have
such a hard time
admitting when
they are wrong ~

Your Thoughts

~ Be so great
that others
feel
inadequate when
they are
near you ~

Your Thoughts

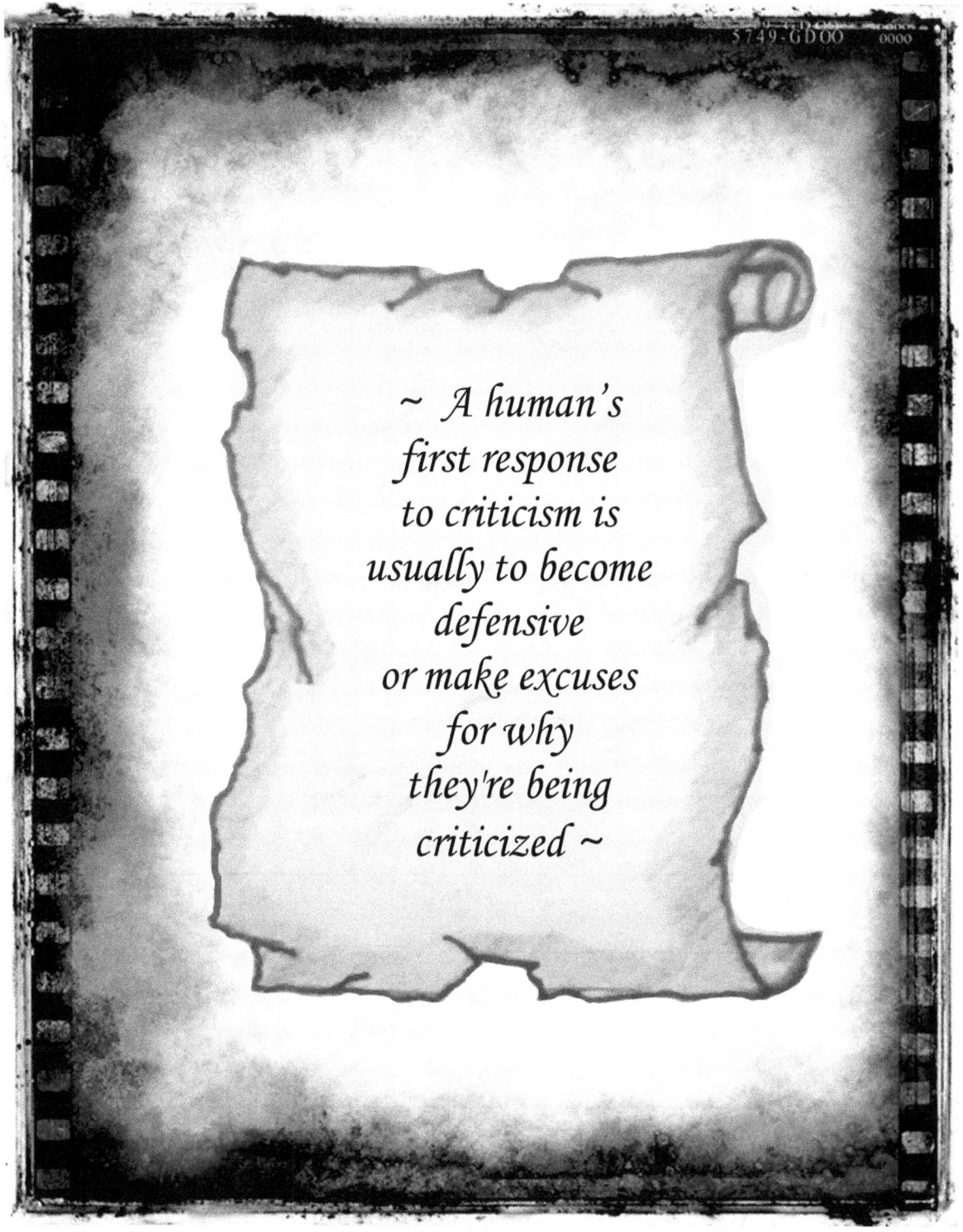

~ A human's first response to criticism is usually to become defensive or make excuses for why they're being criticized ~

Your Thoughts

~ People say "hope for the best, expect the worst". That is a losers mentality. ALWAYS EXPECT THE BEST!!! ~

Your Thoughts

~ *If you're waiting for someone to do the right thing, you'd better have a lot of time on your hands* ~

Your Thoughts

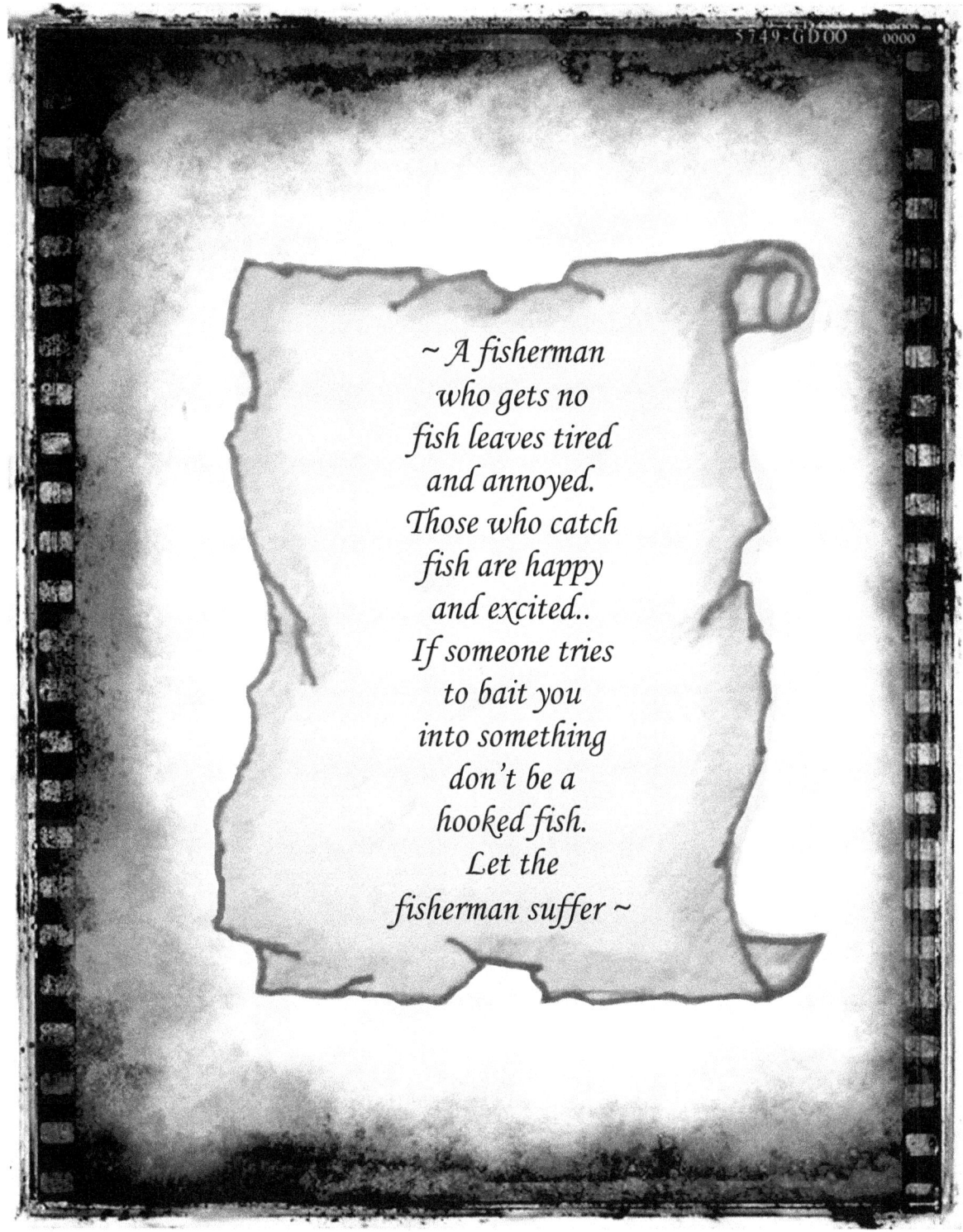

~ A fisherman who gets no fish leaves tired and annoyed. Those who catch fish are happy and excited.. If someone tries to bait you into something don't be a hooked fish. Let the fisherman suffer ~

Your Thoughts

~ Today's society of social media has left an enormous opening for disgusting cowardice. Too many people have the freedom to hurt others while concealing their identity. Anyone can be a tough guy from behind their keyboard, if you can't own up to your comments and say it face to face then keep your coward fingers off the keyboard. P.S. I like to refer to these people as "keyboard cowards" ~

Your Thoughts

~ Quick story, I was leading a warm-up before one particular karate class and instructed the class to do 50 pushups. I noticed one guy who only did 32. So after the warm-ups I pulled him aside and told him " your only making yourself weaker when you cheat". He disagreed and said that 32 pushups was good. I responded with "yes, 32 is good and you are 32 pushups physically stronger than when you walked in. However, you have made yourself mentally weaker by allowing yourself to quit and by doing so your conditioning your mind to give up when things get difficult. So as I said "your making yourself weaker when you cheat" ~

Your Thoughts

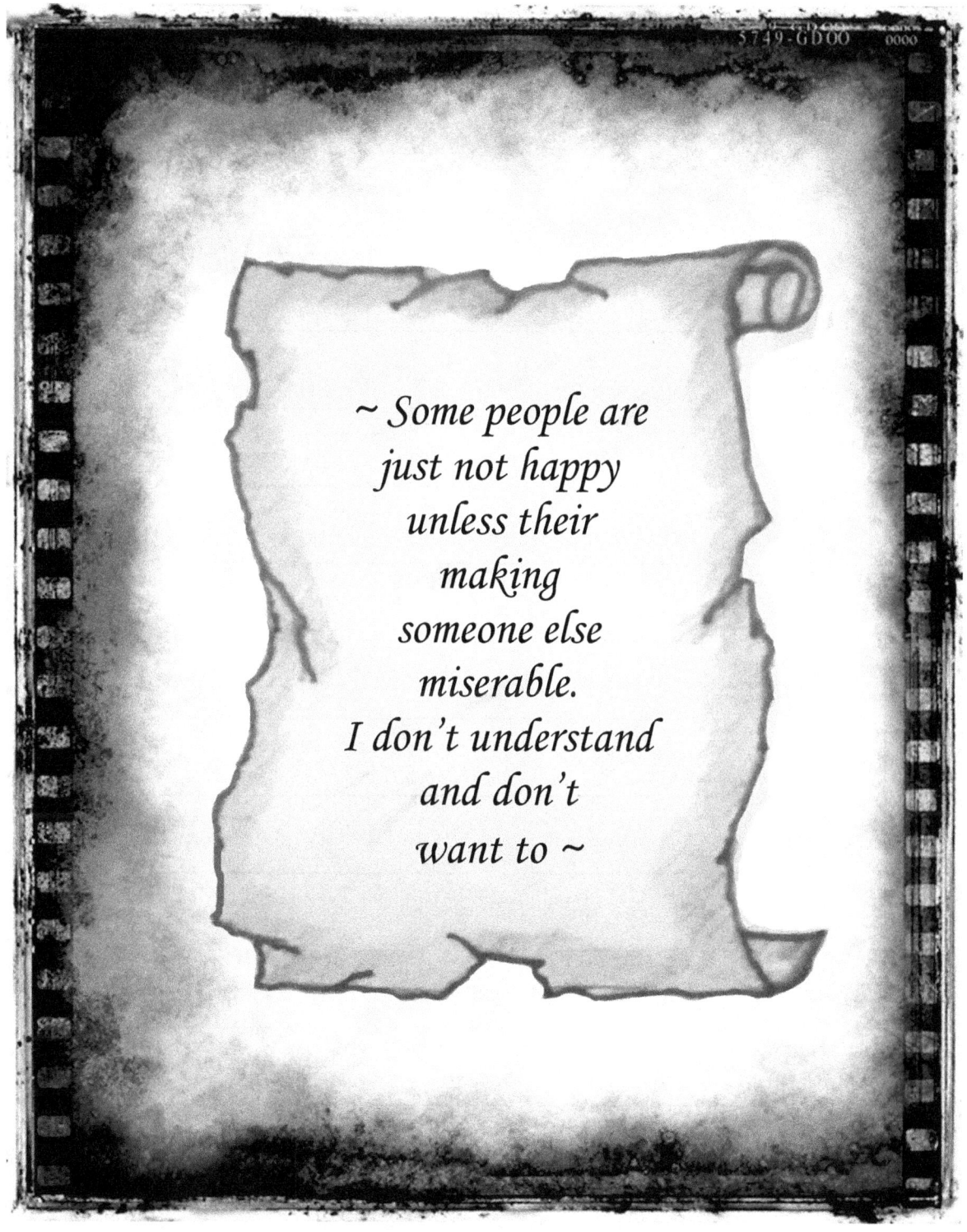

~ Some people are just not happy unless their making someone else miserable. I don't understand and don't want to ~

Your Thoughts

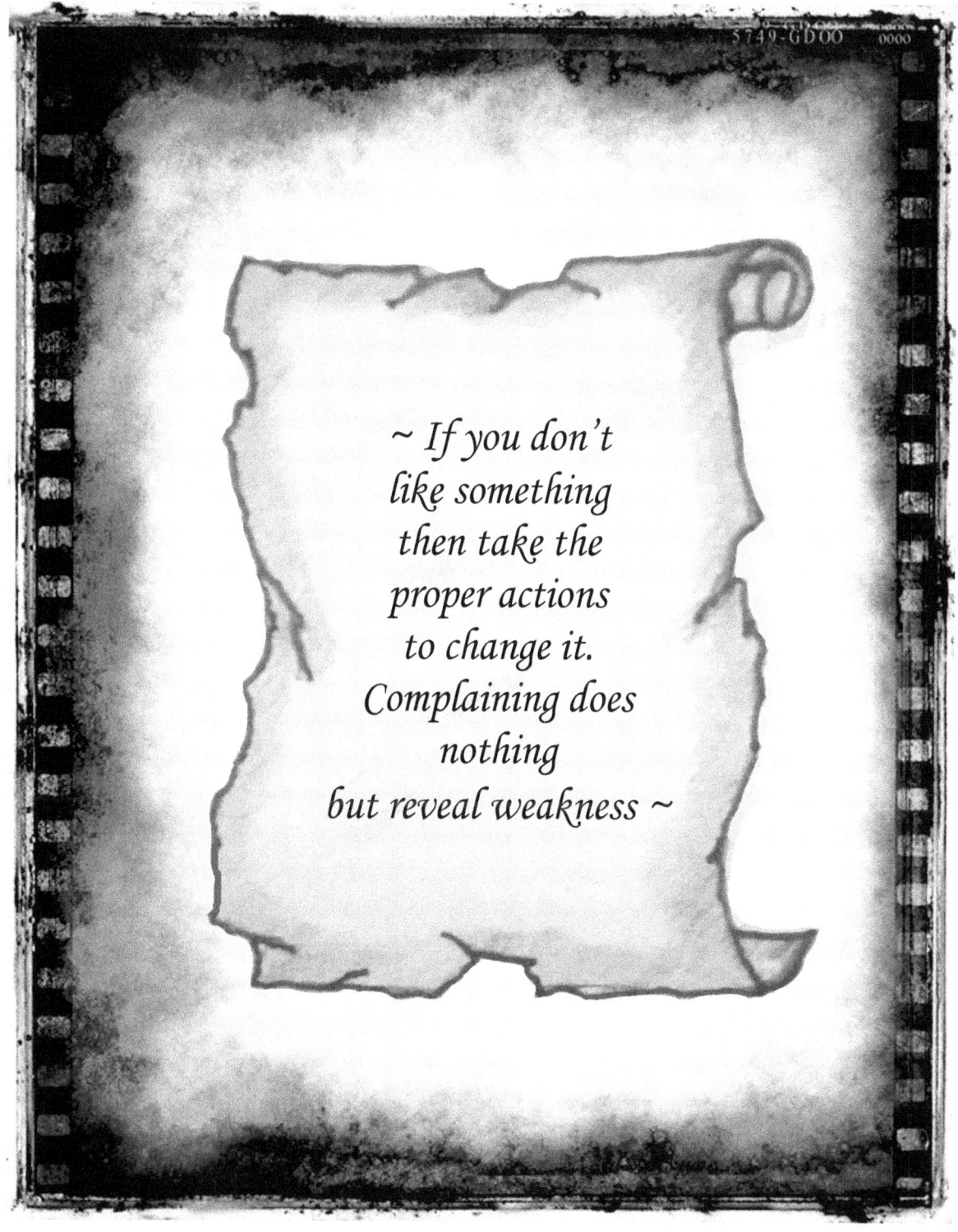

~ If you don't like something then take the proper actions to change it. Complaining does nothing but reveal weakness ~

Your Thoughts

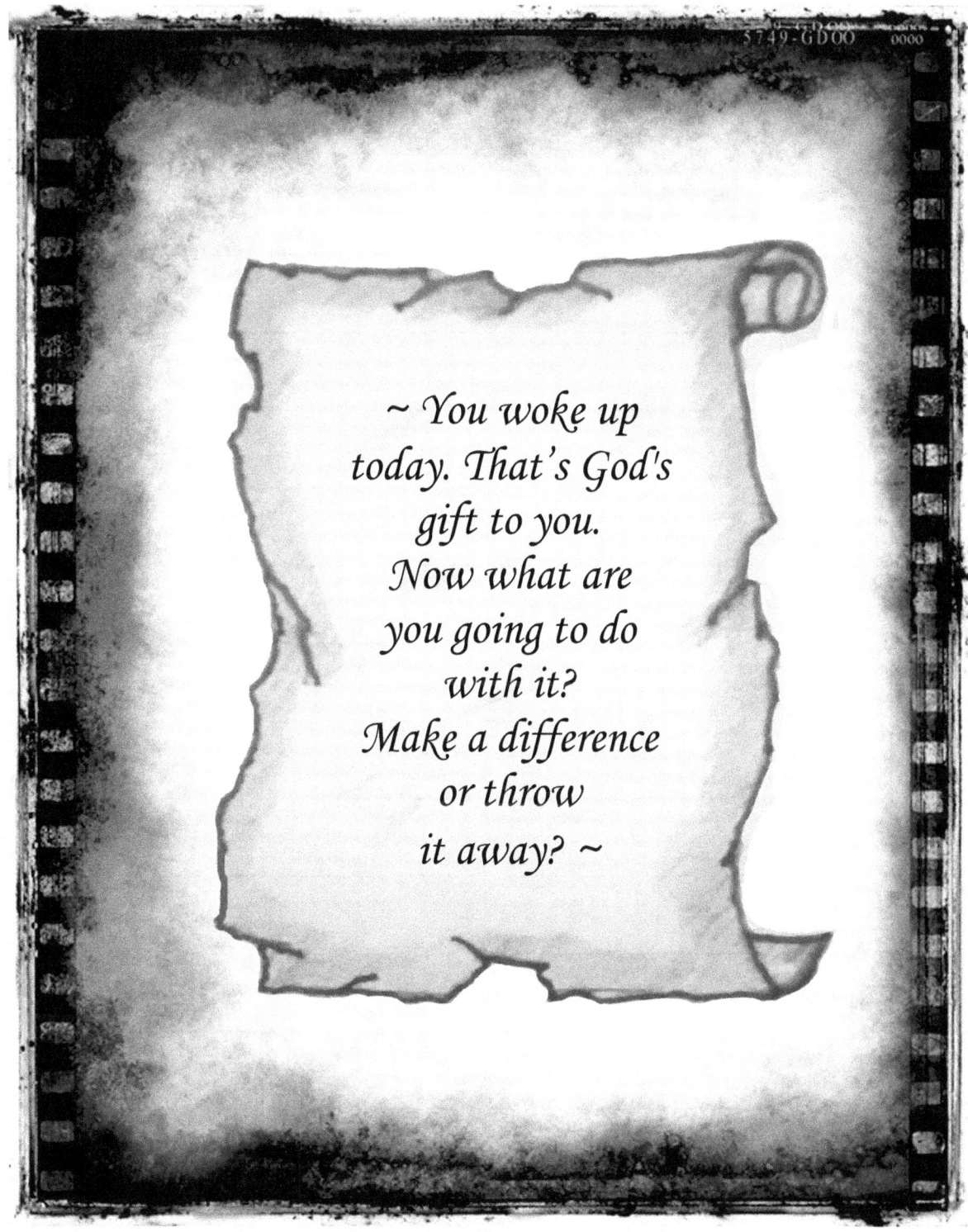

Your Thoughts

~ Every day is another brick. It's up to you to decide whether you build a doghouse or a mansion ~

Your Thoughts

~ The more they laugh, the more jealousy is revealed ~

Your Thoughts

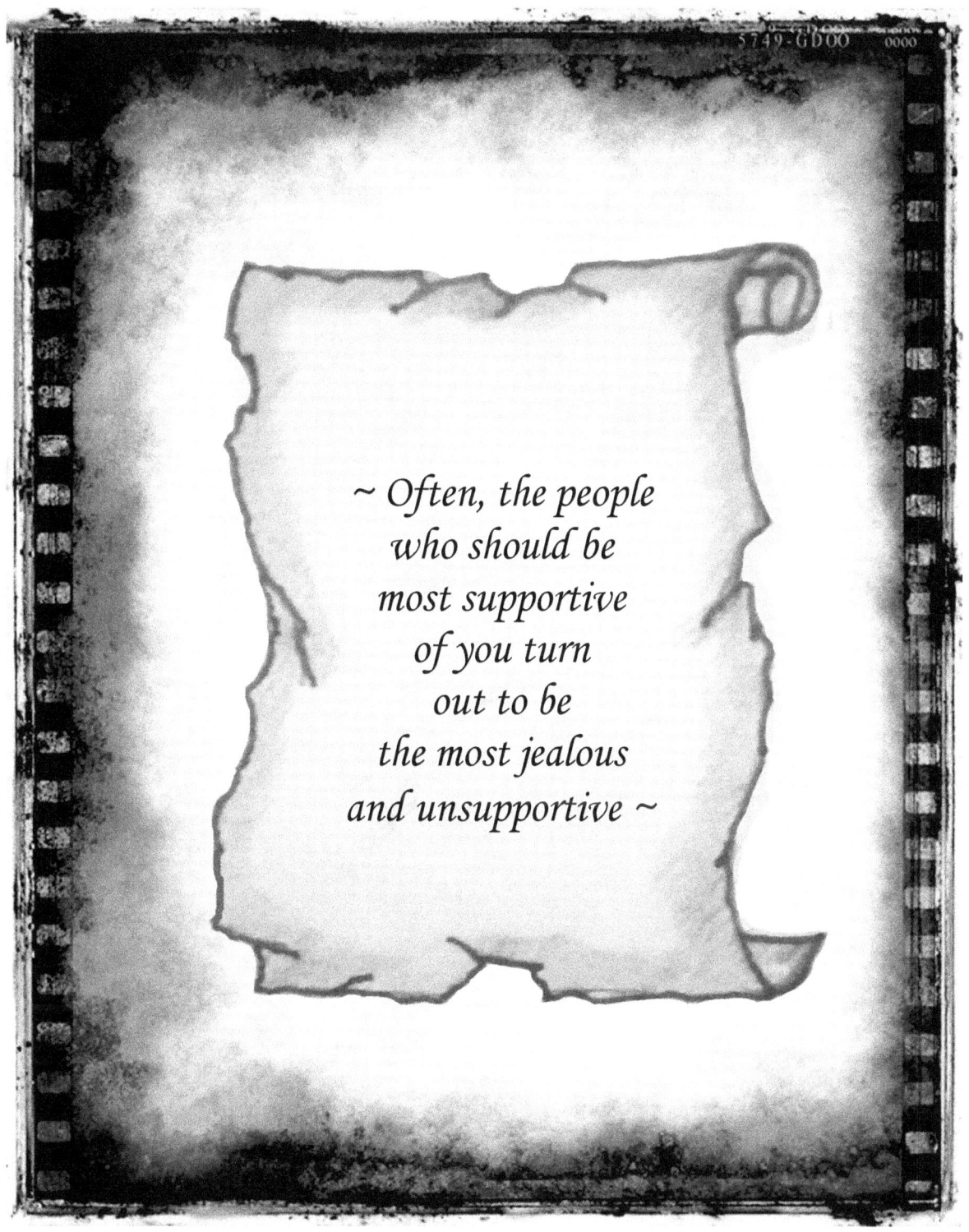

~ Often, the people who should be most supportive of you turn out to be the most jealous and unsupportive ~

Your Thoughts

~ Sometimes you need to break away from those you love because they are the ones holding you back ~

Your Thoughts

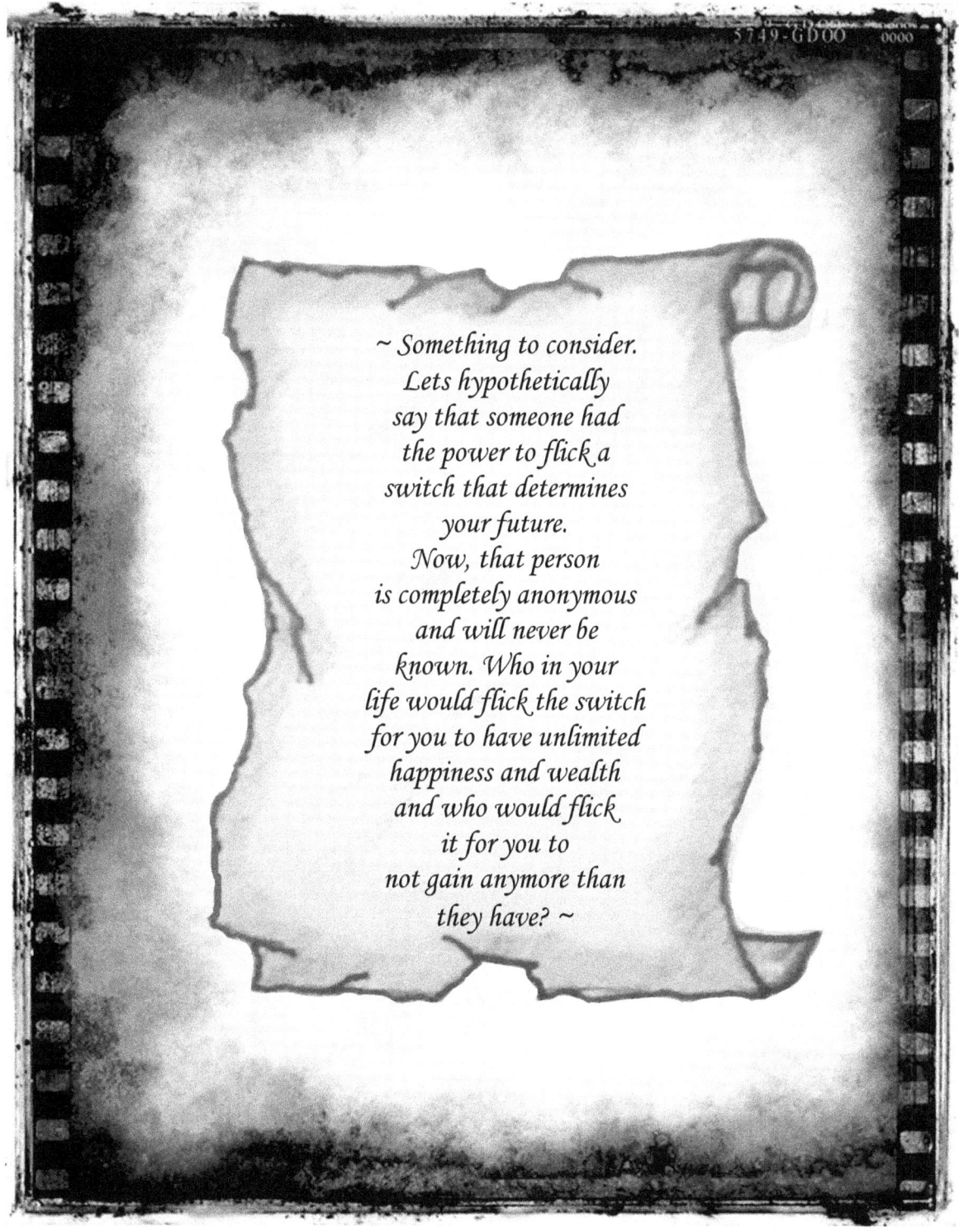

~ Something to consider. Lets hypothetically say that someone had the power to flick a switch that determines your future. Now, that person is completely anonymous and will never be known. Who in your life would flick the switch for you to have unlimited happiness and wealth and who would flick it for you to not gain anymore than they have? ~

Your Thoughts

~ Be careful if you choose to lie. Sometimes the person you lie to may know the truth before even asking the question ~

Your Thoughts

~ One who loses control, loses the battle ~

Thank you for taking this journey through my eyes. Hopefully it was in some way beneficial to you. I think it's easy to become consumed with our own lives and sometimes forget about others or maybe take for granted the little things in life. As a society we need to step back sometimes, look at the big picture and appreciate more and complain less. I myself am guilty of all the same flaws and in no way exclude myself from making mistakes. We are all humans and will never be perfect. However, realizing our errors and trying everyday to correct them and the constant pursuit of being a better person should be our goal. Thank you again and God bless!!

Kevin Hines

www.ingramcontent.com/pod-product-compliance
Lightning Source LLC
Chambersburg PA
CBHW081345040426
42450CB00015B/3310